FROM ZERO TO ROCK HERO

— IN JUST 6 WEEKS! —

FROM ZERO TO ROCK HERO

LEARN HOW TO PLAY ELECTRIC GUITAR IN JUST 6 WEEKS!

OWEN EDWARDS

COLLINS DESIGN

An Imprint of HarperCollins Publishers

First published in the United States and Canada in 2009 by
Collins Design
An Imprint of HarperCollins*Publishers*
10 East 53rd Street
New York, NY 10022
Tel: (212) 207-7000
Fax: (212) 207-7654
collinsdesign@harpercollins.com
www.harpercollins.com

Distributed throughout the United States and Canada by
HarperCollins*Publishers*
10 East 53rd Street
New York, NY 10022
Fax: (212) 207-7654

This book was conceived, designed, and produced by
Quintet Publishing Limited
The Old Brewery
6 Blundell Street
London N7 9BH
UK

Music Editor: Nick Andrew
Audio Recording: Stephen Loveday
Illustrators: Bernard Chau, Paul Wootton
Designer: Ian Ascott
Art Editor: Zoe White
Art Director: Michael Charles
Editorial Assistant: Tanya Laughton
Project Editor: Robert Davies
Managing Editor: Donna Gregory
Publisher: James Tavendale

ISBN: 978-0-06-180994-1

Library of Congress Control Number: 2009927513

Printed in China by 1010 Printing International Limited
First printing, 2009

CONTENTS

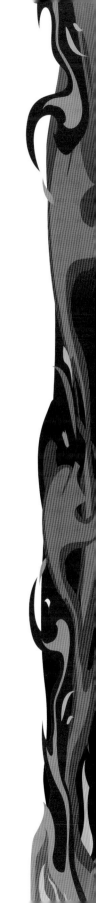

Introduction	6
History of Rock Guitar	8
Chapter One: Mission Brief	10
Chapter Two: Preparing for Battle	28
Chapter Three: Basic Training	40
Chapter Four: Open Chord Riffs	70
Chapter Five: Feel the Power	84
Chapter Six: Let's Rock	106
Chapter Seven: Phrasing Techniques and Hot Licks	118
Chapter Eight: Scales	134
Chapter Nine: What's Been Going on?	144
Chapter Ten: Mixing it Up	158
Chapter Eleven: Time to Burn	178
Index	190
Credits	192

INTRODUCTION

Welcome to the wonderful world of rock guitar—and what a great time to be getting into the most influential, important, and downright coolest instrument of all! Rock music—a style exemplified by everyone from Jimi Hendrix, Led Zeppelin, and Van Halen through to AC/DC, Metallica, and Nickelback—is as vital and popular today as it was back at the dawn of rock in the late 1960s.

Truly it can be said that rock music, arguably above all other genres of music in history, spans generations and cultures. Let's face it, has there ever been a period in time when your parents—and even grandparents—are as likely to be into the same music and bands as you are? When people from the Western world are as fixated by the same bands as someone in the farthest reaches of Nepal?

And what unites them all? The sound of a screaming electric guitar! Unquestionably the most iconic instrument in history, this humble piece of mass-produced wood and steel has supplanted all previous instruments to become not only a musical tool but also a definition of a generation, a statement of what it is to be young (in heart), free, and individualistic. A guitar player doesn't operate by the same rules as your next-door neighbor—they are modern-day troubadours, warriors of the open road, musical cowboys on the open plains of rock. And above them all stands the rock guitar hero.

From Zero To Rock Hero… In Just 6 Weeks is designed to get you on the road to being a rock guitar hero in as short a time as possible: by following this book's program of lessons, advice, and musical examples you can realize your dream of being a bona fide guitar dude in record time.

Above left: the legendary Jimmy Page
Center: stadium rockers Kiss
Below left: tapping genius Eddie Van Halen

Let's look at this in more depth, so you know where I am coming from: from years of teaching privately, at schools, and at guitar workshops I have gained an insight into what it takes to get to a decent level as a rock guitar player. The average student, at best, practices (and by that I mean real practice, not aimless noodling around on the guitar!) for around 30 minutes a day, maximum. That means that the average student will clock up a maximum of about 180 hours per year.

But, say you're at school and have the summer vacation ahead of you—or maybe you are an actor preparing for a role that requires you to be able to play the guitar as quickly as possible: let's just say you have six weeks clear to get to grips with the guitar—just what is feasible in that time?

Well, first of all, approach this like you mean business! Let's take an average working/school day of around 9 hours and multiply it by six weeks: that's 378 hours.

That equates to over two years of "normal" practicing time. OK, here we're including weekends—but hey, rock & roll's not just a day job, it's a lifestyle! Best to get used to that concept now, folks!

Anyway, what all this number crunching means is that theoretically, using the material in this book—and, crucially, applying yourself—you can, over six weeks, get to the standard that most people take a minimum of two years to achieve!

But here's the rub: using this book you won't waste one minute of practice time. Everything here is designed to take you from buying a guitar to performing on stage in record time. So the only thing you have to ask yourself is: have you got what it takes?

Above left: guitar icon Slash
Right: screaming guitar fans

HISTORY OF ROCK GUITAR

Before we jump in let's have a quick look at the history of rock guitar playing and how it has evolved into the musical force that we all love today.

There was no fixed point in time when rock guitar was created—rather, it was a gradual evolution of existing guitar styles that merged into what we now term rock guitar—but it is generally agreed that by the mid-to-late 1960s a new breed of guitar players emerged who were indisputably rock guitar heroes. There were also the technological advances in amplification that created previously unheard tones such as distortion, enabling these players to explore an amazing new musical territory.

In the 1950s early rock & roll, spearheaded by Chuck Berry in the United States, laid the foundations. Then this was combined with the early 1960s electric blues guitar boom, a whole generation of icons such as Eric Clapton, Jeff Beck, Ritchie Blackmore, Jimmy Page, and Jimi Hendrix exploded on the music scene and changed guitar playing forever. These guys were, and still are, rock guitar heroes!

No longer stuck in a sideman role, these players—and the countless others who followed—took center stage, lapping up the adulation of millions of fans all over the world. With massive riffs, exciting solos, and sheer showmanship these guys pushed back the boundaries and laid clear the path for the decade of rock—the 1970s, when rock truly ruled the world.

Whether it was heavy metal, country rock, Southern rock, glam, prog rock, or any of the other subgenres that the late 1960s and early 1970s guitar boom spawned, what was clear was that we were now in the era of heroes—and rock has never looked back!

Above left: Chuck Berry
Left: prog gods Pink Floyd
Right: the iconic Marshall amp
and Gibson Les Paul guitar

In the States, Ace Frehley was tearing up the rulebook in Kiss, The Eagles were producing epic solos that even the country fans freaked to, and down South, Lynyrd Skynyrd and ZZ Top flew the flag. From Europe, Led Zeppelin, Black Sabbath, Deep Purple, Queen, Thin Lizzy, Judas Priest, and The Scorpions—not forgetting Australia's AC/DC—all kept hold of the flame and ensured that the iconic imagery of a Gibson Les Paul, a Fender Strat, and Marshall amp are so enduring now, almost 40 years later.

Then, in late 1970s California, Eddie Van Halen rewrote the guitar's rulebook and heralded the 1980s: a decade of virtuoso rock players, guys who could hack it with the most advanced jazz guitarists technically—but do it with fire, abandon, and excitement that was off the scale. With bands such as Metallica, Guns 'N' Roses, Poison, Mötley Crüe, and Bon Jovi rock flourished as never before.

Throughout the 1990s (Nirvana, Pearl Jam, Soundgarden, and Rage Against The Machine, to name a few) and the 2000s (Marilyn Manson, Slipknot, Linkin Park, etc.) rock guitar continued to evolve and change with the times (whisper it, but there were times during these years when playing a guitar solo was most definitely not cool… although riffs certainly were!) but one thing was always constant: the sound of a rock guitar. Now it seems we are in full circle: almost every rock band has a hot guitarist, solos are back, riffs are aplenty, and the guitar has never been more popular!

So, what are you waiting for? Let's dig straight in and see if you have what it takes to become the next decade's rock hero!

Above: Ace Frehley of Kiss, live onstage in 1975
Left: Deep Purple's Ritchie Blackmore
Right: Slipknot's Mick Thompson
Below: Bon Jovi's Richie Sambora rocking it up in the 1980s

CHAPTER ONE:
MISSION BRIEF

From Zero To Rock Hero is designed to give you the musical and physical tools required to become cool enough on the guitar to perform real rock music to performance level in as short a time as possible. Everything here is focused on developing your rock guitar playing ability—no more and no less. This book is written mainly for the complete beginner, but works equally well for someone who has been playing rock guitar for a while but wants to check they've got all the basics correct and to fill in any areas they are unsure of.

HOW TO USE THIS BOOK

This book is designed to make you a cool rock/metal guitarist: if you want to learn indie, classical, or jazz guitar, this isn't the book for you. But if you want to become a rock guitarist, this will do it in record time.

HOW?

In this book, we've got rid of loads of exercises—like the old-fashioned books and teachers used to make you do—that would bore you and teach you things you'd probably never use again. We are cutting this to the bone so that you can do what you really want to do: start rocking!

Once you can hold a guitar properly, and know roughly what to do with your picking and fretting hands, we will get you straight in there by giving you musical examples that will not only amaze your buddies, but also give you a solid grounding in the techniques rock guitar heroes have used for years. There is no shortcut for hard work—but it sure can be a lot more fun than you might think!

All musical examples have a target week and day number alongside them that you can aim for: this is an easy way for you to track your progress.

Just remember not to get too downhearted if you cannot achieve all these targets—you will find some exercises easier than others, and some will seem impossible to begin with… but stick with it, put the hours in, and you will be amazed at your progress!

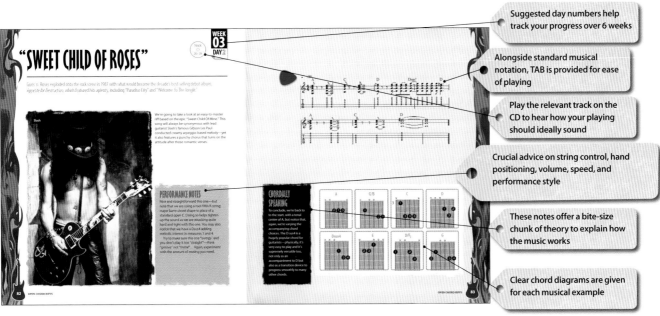

Suggested day numbers help track your progress over 6 weeks

Alongside standard musical notation, TAB is provided for ease of playing

Play the relevant track on the CD to hear how your playing should ideally sound

Crucial advice on string control, hand positioning, volume, speed, and performance style

These notes offer a bite-size chunk of theory to explain how the music works

Clear chord diagrams are given for each musical example

YOUR EQUIPMENT

In order to get your rock chops rolling, you're going to need some good basic gear. The good news is that instruments and amps have never been better value for your hard-earned cash—so you have no excuse for not being able to get a cool rig!

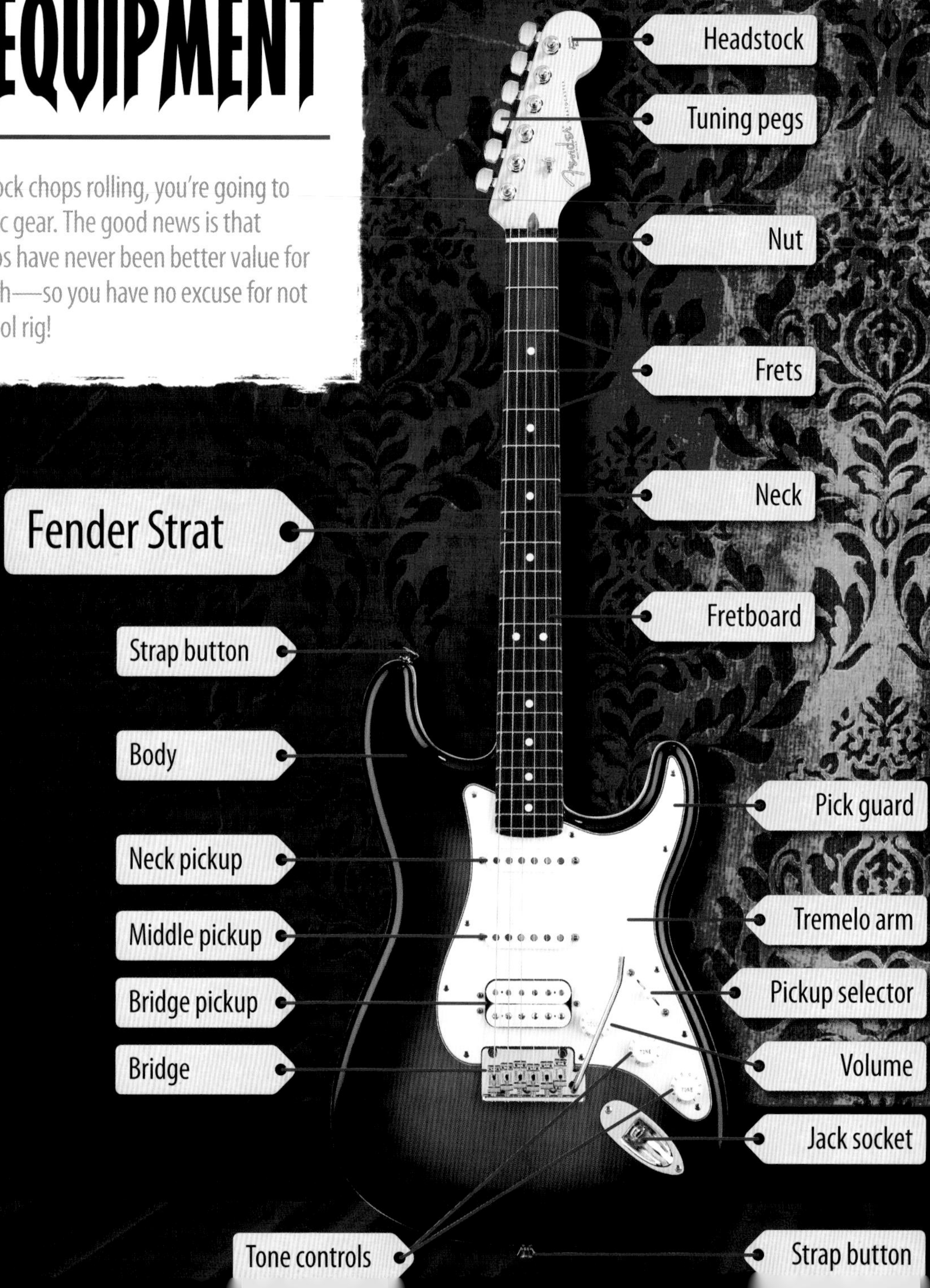

Headstock

Tuning pegs

Nut

Frets

Neck

Fretboard

Fender Strat

Strap button

Body

Neck pickup

Middle pickup

Bridge pickup

Bridge

Pick guard

Tremelo arm

Pickup selector

Volume

Jack socket

Tone controls

Strap button

THE GUITAR

Firstly, and most importantly, the guitar. It may seem obvious to point out, but you are not going to get the most out of this book with an acoustic or classical guitar—sure, you'll be able to make do (and it sure as hell beats playing air guitar!) but if you haven't got an electric guitar already, at some point very soon you will need one!

Although there are many different models out there, most will fall into being basically a Fender Strat type or a Gibson Les Paul/SG type.

Examples of famous Fender players include Jimi Hendrix, Eric Clapton, Yngwie Malmsteen, Ritchie Blackmore (Deep Purple), and many more.

Examples of famous Gibson players include Jimmy Page, Slash, Angus Young (AC/DC), Joe Perry (Aerosmith), Tony Iommi (Black Sabbath), and Ace Frehley (Kiss).

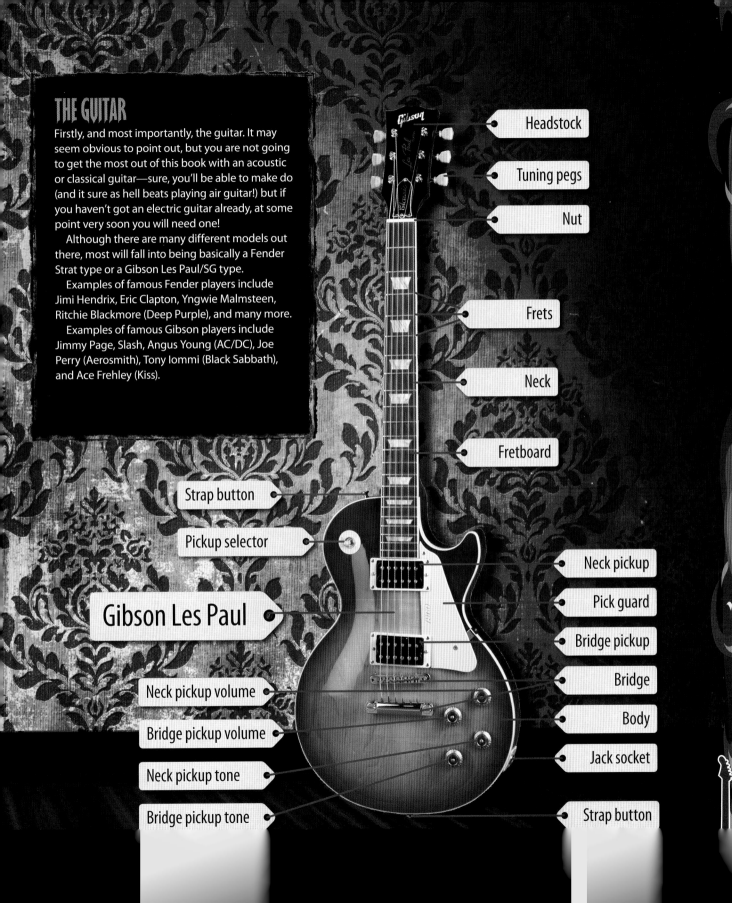

Headstock

Tuning pegs

Nut

Frets

Neck

Fretboard

Strap button

Pickup selector

Gibson Les Paul

Neck pickup

Pick guard

Bridge pickup

Bridge

Body

Jack socket

Neck pickup volume

Bridge pickup volume

Neck pickup tone

Bridge pickup tone

Strap button

DESIGNED TO ROCK

In the late 1970s Eddie Van Halen took a basic Strat and put in Gibson-style humbucker pickups to get a beefier tone, as well as using a Floyd Rose tremolo (a double locking system that cured the standard Strat's trem tuning problems that were incurred by his manic whammy bar use!) to create what became known as a "Super Strat."

In the 1980s companies such as Charvel, Kramer, Jackson, Ibanez, Dean, and ESP all produced guitars in this style—some with wacky and wonderful styling—and these have since become the weapons of choice for virtuoso guitarists including Joe Satriani, Paul Gilbert, and Steve Vai—as well as full-on metalheads such as Kirk Hammet and Dimebag Darrell.

In recent years PRS guitars have been the weapon of choice for bands and guitarists in a massive range of styles, from artists as varied as Carlos Santana, Cradle of Filth, Nickelback, and Linkin Park. The best thing to do is to see which type of guitar your favorite players use, and aim to find a guitar in a similar style that is within your price range (it is probably not advisable to try Slayer-style guitar on a basic Strat copy!).

There are dozens of budget brands producing guitars in a similar style to the above models, and you will find that they should all be perfectly good enough for the first couple of years.

WHAT TO LOOK FOR

There are so many guitar brands out there that it can seem daunting to know where to start—and nowadays even the cheapest models are perfectly decent—but nevertheless it is worth following a few guidelines.

As you're pretty new to the instrument it is a given that you'll probably base your decision on what to buy on what looks good—which is fine, but sometimes the flashiest and coolest-looking ax can play like an old dog, and the roughest, most battered-up plank can play like a dream!

The problem is that you are unlikely to be able to tell the difference yet—so whenever possible, take a friend who can already play to a decent standard with you to try the guitar out.

PRS

Ibanez

BUYING SECONDHAND

Of course your cheapest option is to buy a secondhand ax—whether it's locally or via eBay: again I would advise wherever possible to physically try the guitar out (ideally with your guitar-playing buddy to test it) but if you spot a guitar at a crazy price online then go for it. There's not that much that goes wrong on guitars compared with more hi-tech equipment—and if there are problems they are usually pretty easy to get fixed by taking a trip down to your local guitar store and getting the resident guitar tech to take a look at.

SUPPORT YOUR LOCAL GUITAR STORE!

Unless you find a great deal secondhand or on the web, it often pays in the long run to buy your guitar from your local guitar store: you will be safe in the knowledge that if something is faulty, they should deal with it, and the better guitar stores always make sure that the guitar has had a basic setup to ensure it plays well. In addition, getting to know your local store will mean that they look after you for future purchases—not to mention being a great place to meet other musicians for when you're ready to form a band, or even just to find some other guitarists to jam with.

WHAT'S A SETUP?

A setup is basically like taking your car to the garage for a checkup to ensure it runs smoothly. On the guitar it ensures that the instrument will work properly: that the neck is aligned correctly, action is comfortable, the intonation is accurate, and all the electrics are in good working order.

WHAT'S ACTION?

Action is the term given to describe the height of the strings from the fretboard. If the distance is too great, it will be very tough on the fretting hand, too low, and everything will sound rattly and plain messy… you've got enough to be worrying about when learning the instrument without having to fight the guitar!

More and more people are buying sight unseen from the Internet, as, by and large, online retailers will undercut your local guitar store and save you money. If you are going to go down this route, make sure you keep some cash in reserve to pay for a setup from your local guitar repairman if the guitar arrives and is hard to play. Again, don't rely on your own judgment on this: get a guitar-playing friend to assess if the guitar is cool.

THE AMPLIFIER

After the guitar, your next most important piece of equipment is the amplifier, or "amp." Amps amplify the sound of your guitar. They don't just make it audible, but also massively affect the tone produced—so it is important to get the best possible combination of guitar and amp.

WHAT TO LOOK FOR

First off—it's got to sound cool! Again, always attempt to be able to try the amp before you buy, and bring along your buddy who helped you purchase your guitar. Even better, take your own guitar with you, as the way an amp will sound varies massively depending on what guitar is plugged into it.

The main tonal feature to check for is a decent "clean" sound and a decent "overdrive/gain" sound. There is little point, being a rock guitarist, having an amp that has a bad overdrive sound! Your buddy—who is probably becoming your best friend by now—is again going to be the best judge of this, so listen to his advice. Don't just go for the flashiest-looking piece of kit—after all, it's sound we're dealing with here.

Arguably the brand most synonymous with rock guitar is Marshall, who—along with Peavey, Vox, Roland, Line 6, Laney, Hughes & Kettner, and Crate, to name but a few—all produce great-sounding, great-value amps to suit all budgets: from complete beginner to rock god.

The golden rule here, perhaps even more than with an electric guitar, is to try before you buy. After all, if a guitar plays badly, it can be setup, and if it sounds bad, you can put in better pickups. With an amp, the options for improving the sound are minimal.

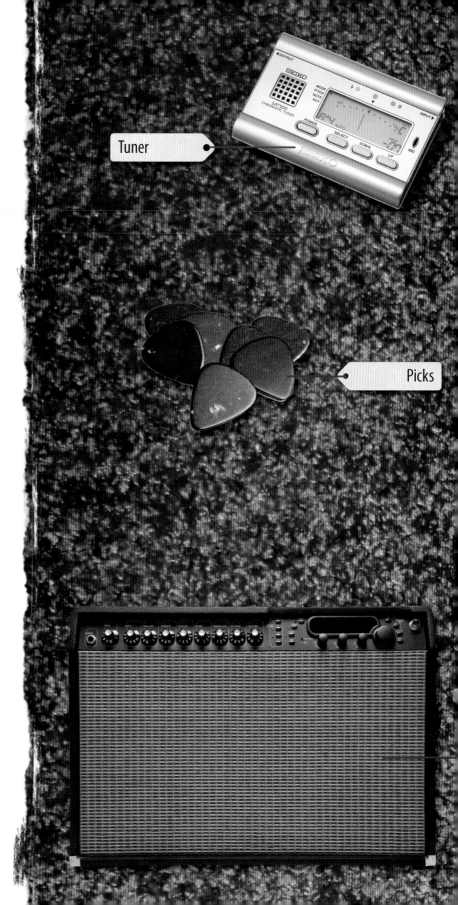

Tuner

Picks

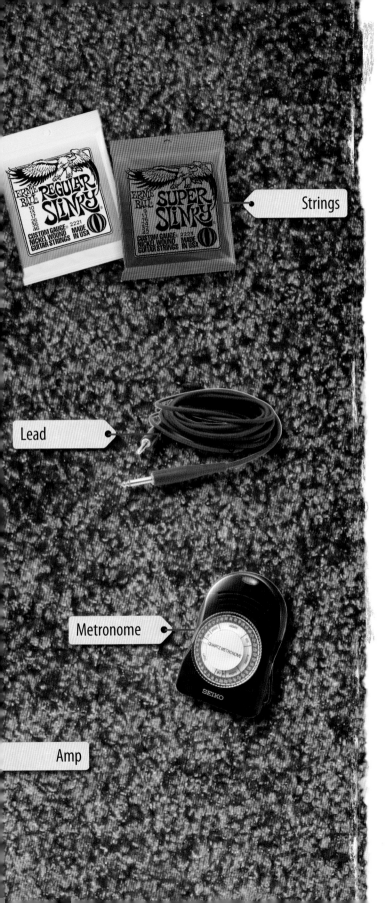

Strings

Lead

Metronome

Amp

PICKS, STRINGS, AND THINGS

Congratulations—you've got your guitar and a cool amp. So what else do you need to get? All too often you'll have blown your budget getting the best guitar and forgotten that you need some more tools to make the things work!

LEADS

Make sure you have a decent lead—i.e., the cable that connects the guitar to the amp. Buy the best quality lead you can. They come in many different lengths; at this stage, it's probably best to go for a lead anywhere between 10 and 20 feet.

STRINGS

The main thing to consider here is string gauge. Gauge refers to the thickness of the strings; the thinner the gauge, the less effort you'll need to apply to fret a note. At this stage, go for the easiest option. Most guitars come factory-supplied with strings; so start with these, and gradually you may be able to go up a gauge: the thicker the string, the better the tone. It's a balancing act between ease of playing and getting a great tone.

PICKS

Too often people grab any old pick—which is a big mistake, as they are pretty vital. You should aim for a pick that is at least $\frac{1}{32}$ inch thick. Dunlop Jazz IIIs are a particular favorite. It may seem easier to start with super-thin picks, but that is a false economy as they will break more regularly and are best suited to gentle acoustic strumming—not rock riffing!

METRONOME

Not the most rock & roll of tools, a metronome helps you keep time by producing a constant beat. These are invaluable to help you develop good timing, and later in the book you will be shown how best to use them. A relatively small amount of time regularly practicing with the aid of a metronome can massively speed up your progress—so file them under "essential!"

TUNER

Don't get those old-fashioned pitch pipes— they are too inaccurate, and rely on a decent set of ears that you won't have developed yet. So turn the page, get your guitar and kit ready, and we will look at using a tuner, as well as a couple of other options.

TUNING THE GUITAR

The first thing you have to be able to do is actually tune your guitar—otherwise all your efforts will be wasted.

Being able to tune your guitar is a hard thing to master, but try it every time you practice and you will become comfortable with tuning. No one finds this easy at first, so don't be demoralized if it takes longer than you think.

Before we start, let's look at the names of the strings. All the exercises and music in this book are using guitars tuned to what is known as "standard tuning." Standard tuning is the most commonly used tuning, but be aware that later on, if you want to play along with some of your favorite bands, you may need to retune the guitar: a lot of heavier bands use "down tuning," which means that the individual strings are tuned lower than standard, as this can add depth and bone-crushing heaviness to songs. "Drop tuning" is also commonly used—but that's something to deal with in the future: most rock songs over the past 40 years or so have used standard tuning, so it's a good place to start!

Fig 1 shows both Fender- and Gibson-style headstocks, the latter also favored by acoustic and classical guitars. The strings are named after the pitch—or note—that they produce when played "open."

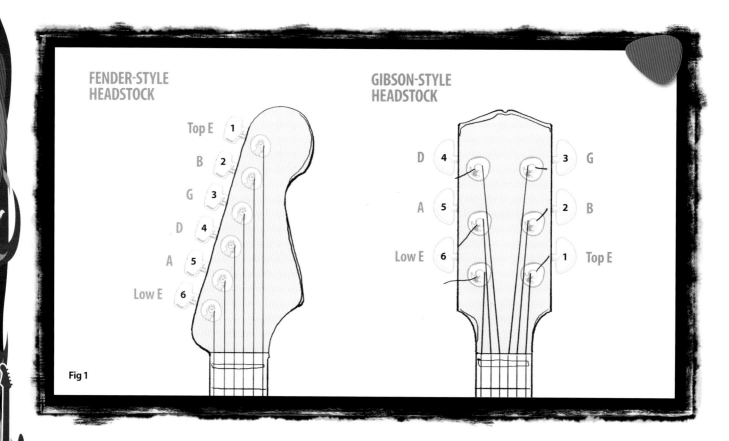

FENDER-STYLE HEADSTOCK

Top E — 1
B — 2
G — 3
D — 4
A — 5
Low E — 6

GIBSON-STYLE HEADSTOCK

D — 4
A — 5
Low E — 6
3 — G
2 — B
1 — Top E

Fig 1

STAGE ONE: USING THE CD

On Track 2 are six tuning notes—these are first the sixth string/low E, then the fifth string/A, up to the first string/top E. Either tighten or loosen the tuning peg until the strings' pitches are as close to the CD notes as your ears will let you achieve. Don't worry if they are not perfect—they almost certainly won't be! Just try it every time you start a practice session, and in time your ears will develop the ability to hear whether you are in tune or not. Having done this, it is a good idea to double check using relative tuning.

STAGE TWO: RELATIVE TUNING

This is a great ear development exercise: get used to trying this before using an electronic tuner as it will help train your ears still further, with the added advantage of helping you to start mentally processing where the notes exist on the fretboard.

The basic principle (Fig 2) is using the tuning notes try to get the sixth string/low E as close to the CD as possible to the first tuning note. Not surprisingly, that note is E.

Now fret (i.e., press down) the fifth fret. This produces the note A which, as luck would have it, is the desired pitch of the fifth string.

Play the initial note (which here should be close to the pitch A) and concentrate on the pitch intently. Stop the string from vibrating to silence it, then play the string directly below (in this instance the fifth string). As already stated, that string's desired pitch is A. As with using the CD, either tighten or loosen the tuning peg until the pitches are as close to each other as your ears will let you achieve. By continuing this through each pair of strings you should by now be getting pretty close! However, before starting to play, check your work with a tuner.

STAGE THREE: USING A TUNER

You're strongly advised to get an electronic tuner. Gradually your ears will develop the ability to hear whether you are in tune or not—but until then, you will need to rely heavily on a tuner. It is worth noting that even the top professionals use tuners nowadays as a matter of course—so it is no disgrace to use one!

Make sure you read the instructions, but most tuners rely on the same basic principle: plug the guitar into the tuner and, making sure that the guitar's volume is on 10, pick each of the strings in turn. The display will indicate if the string is too flat (see Fig 3) or too sharp (see Fig 4). Either tighten or loosen the tuning peg until the arrow is central—and normally the display will light up to let you know you are in tune.

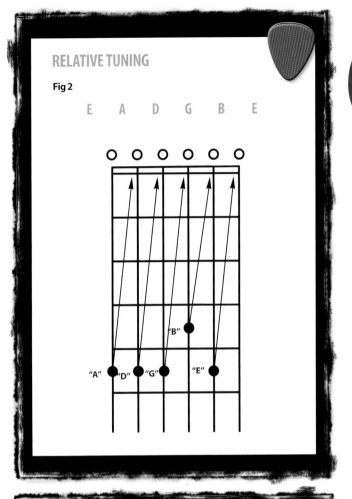

RELATIVE TUNING

Fig 2

E   A   D   G   B   E

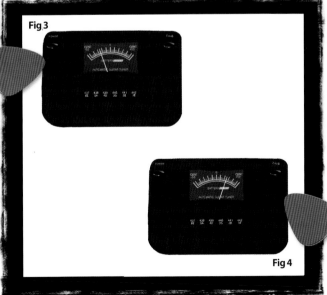

Fig 3

Fig 4

WHAT IS MUSIC MADE OF?
AND WHERE ARE THE NOTES ON THE GUITAR?

Music is made up of differing pitches—referred to as notes from here on—and rhythm. When these two tools are combined, the end result is what we refer to as music.

In Western music there are 12 notes, which are named after the first seven letters of the alphabet—A, B, C, D, E, F, and G. Some of these have sharps and flats between them. This can be a matter of confusion for those learning the guitar, so in order to explain it, let's—weirdly enough—look at a diagram of a keyboard!

You will notice that between A and B, C and D, D and E, F and G, and finally G and A, there are additional black notes—these are those tricky-to-remember sharps or flats, which are notated as ♯ (sharps) and ♭ (flats).

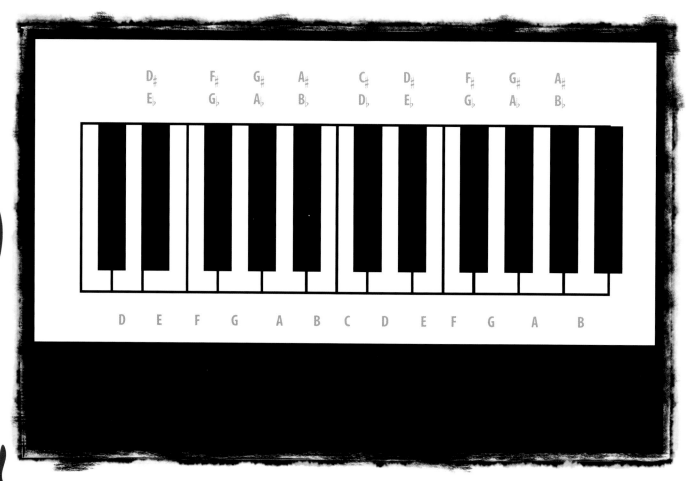

THE NOTES ON THE FRETBOARD

The following diagrams show where the notes are on each of the strings. Learn one string at a time, starting with the sixth/low E string. When you have a good idea of where the notes are on this string, progress to the fith/A string, and continue this process a string at a time.

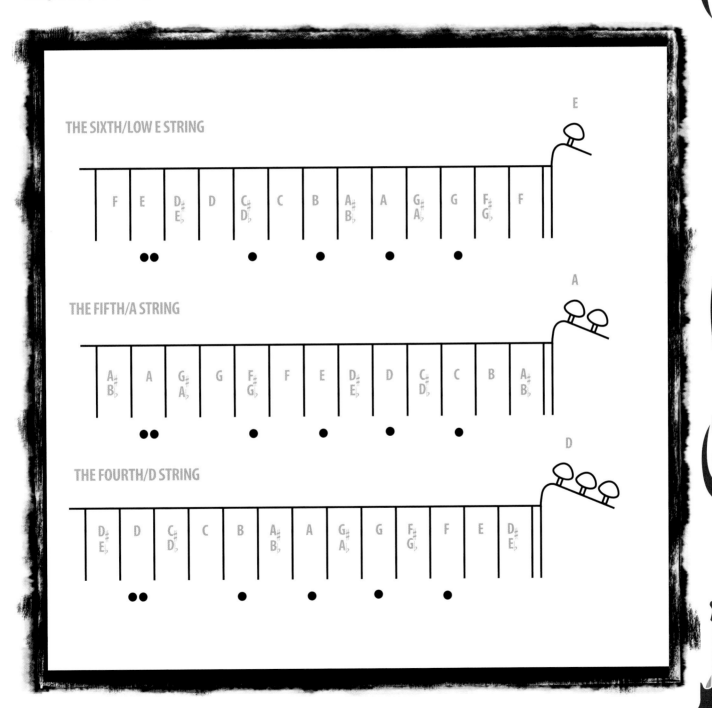

A good exercise is to practice locating a note on the sixth/low E string and then find that same note on the fifth/A string. Do this for a few minutes each day and in no time you will memorize the fretboard. Practice this for each group of adjacent strings—so get cool with the sixth and the fifth strings, then the fifth and the fourth, the fourth and the third, and so on.

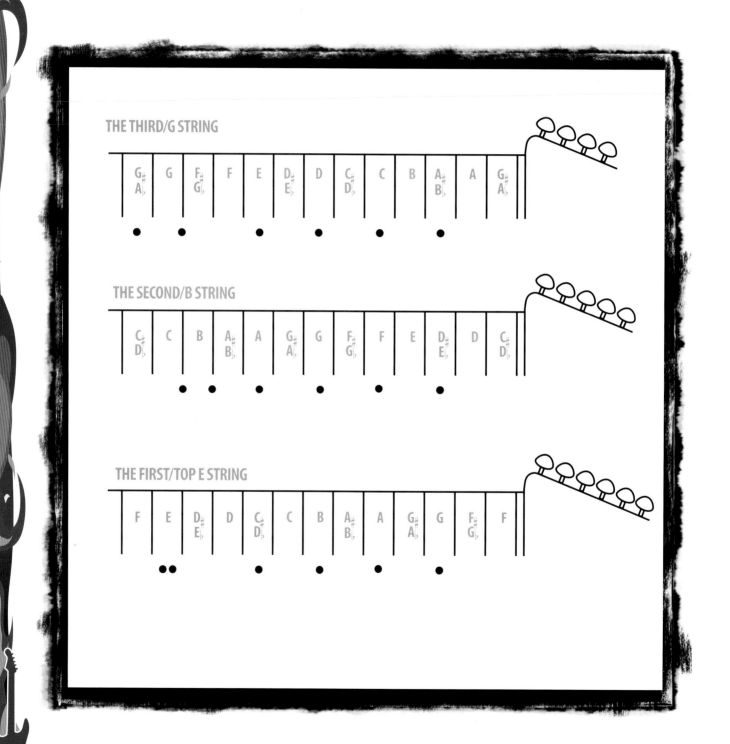

TAB, CHORD, AND SCALE DIAGRAMS

This book uses TAB, standard music notation, chord, scale, and arpeggio diagrams, all in conjunction with music examples on the accompanying CD so you can hear as well as see everything clearly.

WHAT IS TAB?

TAB, short for tablature, is a system you may already be familiar with, as the vast majority of Internet guitar music is written in TAB. It is a basic system that suits all fretted instruments, and is based on a simple graphical representation of six horizontal lines that represent the six strings of the guitar.

A number on any of the horizontal lines refers to the fret you must press down in order to sound a note. Listen to the riff on track 3 and here it is in basic TAB form.

That's it! It's very simple to master, once you've got over the fact that the horizontal lines are arranged in order of the strings' pitch: the lowest line is the sixth string/low E, the top line refers to the first string/top E, etc.

A common beginner's mistake is to assume that the horizontal lines refer to the physical placement of the strings, which is in fact opposite. Remember that we are dealing with sound and pitch and you will see the logicality of having the lowest pitches/strings being represented by the lowest lines and so forth. It also brings the system in line with standard notation—the "old-fashioned" system of musical notation that all those classical dudes have used for centuries.

STANDARD NOTATION

First—don't panic! For the purposes of using this book, reading music is not required—after all, everything is shown in TAB as well as being played on the CD. However, it is still useful to have a basic idea about what all those dots and squiggles actually mean. Learning how to read music brings many benefits—not least of which is the ability to communicate music to other instruments (after all, there's little point in showing a keyboard player TAB)—but there is no doubt it's a daunting and time-consuming task that is beyond the scope of this book.

However, it is worth taking the time now to try to grasp the main advantage that traditional notation has over TAB—the ability to notate rhythm. Basically, TAB is great for guitarists because it shows you exactly where to play any given note, but what it doesn't do is tell you for what length of time you should hold that note—or indeed when you need to silence the instrument. These periods of silence in music are known as rests.

Fig 3 (overleaf) shows the riff we've already listened to on track 3, including traditional notation as well as TAB.

Exercise 1

As already stated, we are not going to learn how to read music in this book, but there are some things you need to be aware of. First of all music is arranged into measures (also known as bars)—Exercise 1, for example, has 4 measures. When you work through the examples in the book you will notice that the "dots" vary in style—some are solitary, some are arranged in groups, some have stems etc.—because their function is not only to display pitch but also to show how long the notes need to be sounded for.

Equally, there are corresponding symbols to indicate the rests which differ according to the length of silence required. There are rest symbols at the end of measures 2 and 4 in Exercise 1. The diagram below shows the rest and note lengths that you are likely to encounter in this book. It is not necessary to memorize or learn these now—just be aware that these symbols do have a purpose. It would be very beneficial for you to look carefully at the musical notation as well as the TAB when working through the musical examples in this book. By the time you get to the end, the symbols should have lost much of their mystique.

NOTE	DURATION	REST
𝅝	Whole note 4 BEATS	▬
𝅗𝅥.	Dotted half note 3 BEATS	▬.
𝅗𝅥	Half note 2 BEATS	▬
𝅘𝅥.	Dotted quarter note 1 ½ BEATS	𝄽.
𝅘𝅥	Quarter note 1 BEAT	𝄽
𝅘𝅥𝅮	Dotted eighth note ¾ BEAT	𝄾.
𝅘𝅥𝅮	Eighth note ½ BEAT	𝄾
𝅘𝅥𝅯.	Dotted sixteenth note ⅜ BEAT	𝄿
𝅘𝅥𝅯	Sixteenth note ¼ BEAT	𝄿

CHORD BOXES

A chord is three or more different notes played at the same time, and using chord boxes is the quickest and easiest way to learn them.

Fig 3 shows the top end of a standard Strat-style guitar, and alongside the guitar diagram a box that represents the strings in vertical lines and the frets in horizontal ones.

Fig 3

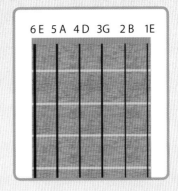

Fig 4 shows a D major and an E minor chord.

- The circles indicate where you should press down your fingers to "fret" a note.
- The numbers within the circles indicate which finger of your fretting hand you should use.
- An O above one of the vertical lines mean that you should also sound that string.
- An X above one of the vertical lines means that you should not play that string.

Fig 4

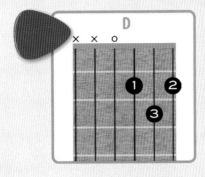
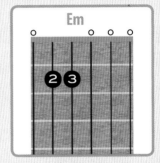

Notice that the D major chord is shown simply as D. This is just musical shorthand to save having to write out the word "major." The E minor chord is shown simply as "Em"—again, musical shorthand. From now on in this book, this is how we will refer to major and minor chords—and it's the system you'll find adopted in all other books, magazines, and websites. First up is the D, followed by the Em. Below, Exercise 2 shows the chords in TAB and standard notation.

TRACK
04

Exercise 2

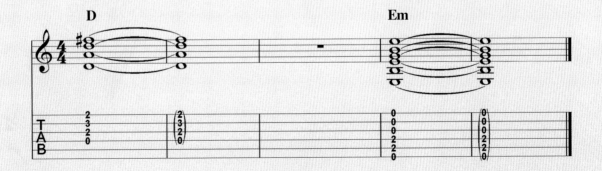

When you're comfortable with the basic shapes, try playing along with the CD.

SCALE DIAGRAMS

A scale is a series of different notes (five or more) organized into a set sequence.

In this book the same basic principle as chord diagrams will apply, with one important variation. Contrary to some other books and magazines, I have found that the most logical way to graphically lay out scales and arpeggios is to arrange them so that the horizontal lines now refer to the strings, and the vertical lines refer to the frets.

WHY THE CHANGE?

It's simply because many scales and arpeggios span more frets than most chords—also, viewing them as a lateral shape rather than a vertical one helps prepare you for the day when you will be playing cool licks up and down the neck rather than being fixed in a set position.

Fig 5 shows an A minor pentatonic scale in diagram form.
• The black circles represent the root notes; in this example, A.
• The empty circles represent the other notes of the scale.
• The number underneath represents the fret you play the shape at.

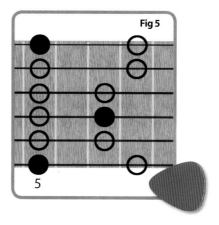

Fig 5

5

Exercise 3 is the corresponding TAB and notation, which you can hear played as shown on track 5.

TRACK
05

Exercise 3

ARPEGGIO DIAGRAMS

An arpeggio is the notes of a chord played separately (normally in succession, either from the lowest to the highest or vice versa).

Fig 6 shows a two-string A minor arpeggio.

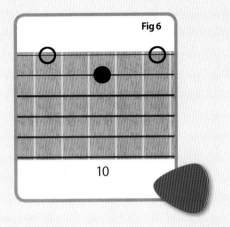

Fig 6

10

Finally, Exercise 4 is the corresponding TAB and notation, which you can hear on Track 6.

TRACK
06

Exercise 4

Arch Enemy's guitarist Christopher Amott (pictured below) performs onstage at El Teatro Theater in Buenos Aires, Argentina.

Rock guitarist practices power chords

CHAPTER TWO:
PREPARING FOR BATTLE

Now you've got your gear sorted out and have an understanding of reading TAB, standard notation, chord, scale, and arpeggio diagrams, we need to address the physical properties of playing the guitar.

HOW TO HOLD THE GUITAR

Many of the biggest mistakes aspiring guitarists make are often down to holding the instrument incorrectly and having inefficient left- and right-hand playing positions.

SEATED

In the real world, a lot of the time you'll be practicing the guitar sitting down. The most common way to hold the guitar is to balance the guitar on your right thigh (or vice versa if you're left-handed), as shown in Fig 1.

Fig 1

Fig 2

- Always sit on an upright chair, preferably without arm rests. Avoid practicing on your bed or a soft or reclining chair—these encourage slouching and you'll end up with your arms tucked into your body.
- Aim to keep both arms free and uninhibited. Keep the guitar neck angled above the parallel—i.e., toward the ceiling as opposed to angled toward the floor. This will get you used to the approximate angle it will be when you are playing standing up, and has the added advantage of having the fretboard closer to head height and thus eye level: as a beginner guitarist you will spend a lot of time looking at the fretboard. It also has the advantage of not encouraging you to lean your forearm on your thigh (see Fig 2).
- Try to avoid leaning over too much. Keep your back straight, your head upright, and your chest out. This promotes good posture and diminishes the chances of back pain and neck ache when you are practicing for prolonged periods. Again, Fig 2 shows what is not desired.
- Don't forget to breathe! Seriously: many students, when practicing and concentrating hard, tense up and hold their breath when playing—not desirable!
- Finally, relax—there can be a real tendency to tense up the forearms and wrists, and this will just end up in stiff and uncomfortable sounding music.

STANDING

Since you're holding this book and reading these words, it's a fair assumption to make that you want to play in a band at some point—so you should strive to get used to playing standing up as soon as possible: how about today?

First of all let's touch on how high, or low to adjust the strap height to hold the guitar. Look at some of the most iconic rock guitarists in history such as Led Zeppelin's Jimmy Page, Aerosmith's Joe Perry, and Guns 'n' Roses' Slash: they are all known for holding their guitars exceptionally low. Why? Image—this low slung position enables that cool 'n' sassy look when strutting across a stadium concert stage—but this is not the best way to hold the guitar when you are starting to learn: it accentuates acute wrist angles and makes the instrument a lot harder to play.

The basic fact is that the higher (within reason!) you hold the guitar the easier it is to play, the lower you hold it the harder it gets. Logically then, we all should adopt a high playing position… but for many music styles (particularly punk rock!) holding the guitar higher just looks plain wrong! What you need to do is balance ease of playing with "coolness"—so experiment with differing playing heights until you find one that you are comfortable with and follow these basic guidelines.

The basic rules are the same as for when you are practicing sitting down, but also note:

- Avoid slouching and leaning your head too far down.
- Make sure that your wrists are at a relaxed angle (particularly your fretting hand). It should never hurt when practicing (apart from, initially, your fingertips—it will take a while to build up the calluses and toughen the skin).
- Practice in front of a mirror: if it looks awkward it's probably wrong—so aim to adopt a relaxed pose, and pretty soon the guitar should begin to feel like a natural extension of your body.
- Don't have the guitar too low—even if your role models are guitarists who play with the guitar down around the knees. They have been playing for years and can pull off what is required, even though they are adopting an inefficient pose. You are new to this, and it's going to be tough enough to master basic playing without imposing extra difficulties.
- Equally, if you do insist on adopting a low-slung god pose from day one, master your playing at a medium height and then gradually lower your ax a notch at a time until you begin to feel strain. By gradually conditioning your body you will, in time, attain a genuine rock god posture, so be patient. Just remember never to force it!
- Finally, relax, relax, and relax! Tension is the number one enemy to good playing.

Fig 3

FRETTING-HAND POSITIONING
CHORDS AND ARPEGGIOS

Now we've got you holding the guitar correctly, let's turn our attention to how to position your hands.

When playing chord-based songs and riffs, your fretting hand needs to adopt a much more arched position than when playing more scale-based licks and riffs. This is because you will often need two or more strings to be able to ring together at the same time.

When fretting the individual strings of a chord, you will need to adopt a fingertip-based approach, with your fingers arched away from the fretboard so that each string can ring freely without being muted. Fig 1 shows this clearly and displays the Em chord we looked at in Chapter One.

Fig 1

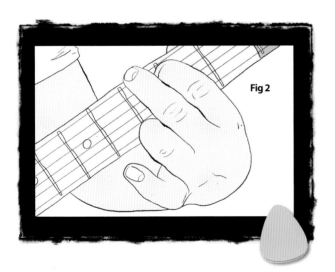

Fig 2

You should aim to have your fingers and hand angle fairly straight—almost parallel with the angle of the frets, as shown in Fig 2.

To double check that your hand is arched enough to allow all the strings to ring clearly, also pick out each of the strings individually: playing a chord in this manner is known as playing an "arpeggio."

PICKING-HAND POSITIONING
CHORDS AND RIFFS

Most of your time will be almost solely devoted to rhythm guitar playing—and a vast majority of this will require your picking hand to be strumming power chord- and chord-based riffs, so let's get you started on this.

Power chords and chords are simply two or more strings/notes played together at the same time, as opposed to melody lines or licks, which are generally based on scales and involve successive single notes.

Effective playing of chords and scales necessitates different fretting-hand/arm positioning. What works best for one invariably doesn't work for the other—so you'd better get used to this now and save yourself a lot of work along the road.

Strumming is the term given to hitting several strings at once in a single flowing movement, using a combination of down strokes and up strokes and ideally involves a relaxed motion that comes from almost the entire arm. Fig 1 shows a standard strumming position. Notice that the heel of the picking hand is "floating," and your forearm is clearly away from the body of the guitar. Fig 2 shows the same technique, viewed from the front of the guitar.

When strumming chords, your picking hand and arm need to be unhindered, so the arm can move freely and without disruption. This is essential to gain a natural and "free" rhythmic approach.

Now try the now familiar E minor chord, and strum this gently, making sure you connect with all the strings. Avoid the natural tendency to sweep your hand away until you are sure all the strings have sounded.

Problems can arise when executing riffs and songs that require you both to strum and to execute single-note runs within a single phrase. For the parts of a song/riff that require you to strum, simply adopt the techniques shown here, and for the single-note parts of the song/riff, refer to the next two pages. Eventually you will find you will naturally compensate for whatever is required, but to save time in the long run, it is a great idea to be aware of this now, so you can begin to acclimatize yourself.

Fig 1

Fig 2

PICKING-HAND POSITIONING
SCALES AND SINGLE-NOTE LINES

Later in the book you will encounter many lines constructed predominantly from scales, particularly in solos and melody playing. The fretting hand needs to adopt a very different basic playing position when executing these to when you are bashing out chords and most riffs.

The main thing you need to understand is that your picking hand's role is not only to pick whichever string you happen to be playing but also to control string noise—particularly as you will almost invariably be using distortion.

First of all stand in front of a mirror and prepare to pick a single note on the top E string. Ideally, your picking hand should look something like Figs 1 and 2.

Notice that the hand smoothly follows the forearm and there are no sharp angles at the wrist, and the pick is striking the string fairly close to the end of the fretboard. While this isn't essential, having the pick attack the string at this point has two advantages—it provides a fuller tone than farther back toward the bridge, and it encourages the heel and palm of the hand to rest on the other strings, which has great benefits in suppressing noise.

Fig 1

Fig 2

Shown from these angles, you can see how the heel and palm of the hand rests on the other strings and how your hand should smoothly follow the angle of your forearm.

Notice that the heel of your hand is anchored on the bass strings in order to stop them from ringing out. Having your hand resting on the strings gives you a platform or pivot position on the guitar so that you can more accurately apply the pick to your desired string.

Think about the way you write with a pen (an admittedly unusual task in this hi-tech age!)—if the base of your hand is floating above the paper, the only contact you have is with the tip of the pen, which is unstable: this will definitely ensure your writing is messier than your normal approach. The same is true for playing single-string lines—by having a "platform" to rest on you gain massive directional accuracy: and the great side effect is that you control all those pesky strings that have no place in being heard here!

THE "FLOATING" POSITION

Fig 1 shows the less desired "floating" position that many players adopt initially. This is great for rhythmic strumming but painfully inaccurate—and prone to massive excess string noise—when trying your cool solo lines.

A lot of very renowned players can get by with this "floating" position, often in conjunction with using the third or fourth fingers resting on the pick guard below the pickups.

This can work if you are very diligent with the heel of your hand still resting on the bass strings, but this isn't the easiest of positions to adopt. Many players who play in this manner succeed in spite of—not because of—utilizing this approach to playing.

Learning how to solo is hard enough, so why not from save yourself from a lot of hard work and try for the most efficient technique from Day One? That way you can get rockin' quicker!

Fig 1

This shows an awkward picking-hand position— one to avoid.

FRETTING-HAND POSITIONING
FOR SCALES/SINGLE-NOTE LINES

Remember that arched position your fretting hand has to adopt for chords? Well guess what—you've got to do almost the opposite to effectively play scales cleanly.

This boils down to the need for control and muting of the strings. To demonstrate this, let's look at a seemingly straightforward task: playing the fifth fret of the third/G string with your index finger. Now look at your hand's position in a mirror. Fig 2 is what you should aim for, with the base of the index finger/knuckle in contact with the bottom of the neck at around the third fret area, making it necessary for you to angle your index finger to fret the fifth fret of the G string. Notice that your thumb's pad is resting on the top of the neck, providing a basic platform which provides stability. Looked at head on you will notice that your hand and fingers (particularly the index finger) have a lazier and more relaxed position and angle.

Fig 3 shows what is less advisable—a straight-on angle parallel with the frets, with no physical contact with the bottom of the neck. This is very similar to what's generally best for chords.

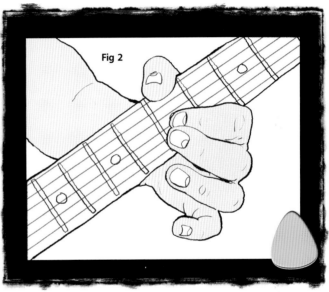

Fig 2

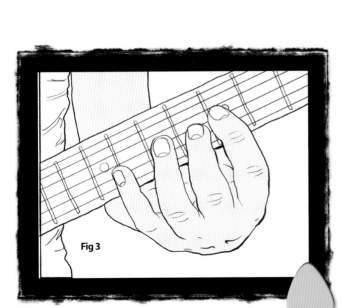

Fig 3

Is that all, then? Afraid not… The thing is, everything on the guitar depends upon the situation that you are in at any given time. Generally, if you are playing single-note lines on the treble strings, adopt the hand position shown in Fig 2. However, if something requires a large stretch—four or more frets on the treble strings— you may need to adopt a more parallel-to-the-frets angle, with your thumb in the middle of the back of the neck to enable your fingers to achieve a wide stretch.

It is also the case, if you are playing scale-type riffs on the bass strings, that your thumb will need to be lower (which will automatically mean your fingers adopt a more parallel-to-the-frets angle) to counter the mass of the neck.

But rest assured, for most scale-based music—particularly licks, solos, and anything that requires bending and vibrato (don't worry, we'll deal with these exotic phrases and techniques later in the book!)—if you follow the basic guidelines as described in the first paragraph and in Fig 2, you'll be ahead of the game!

MUTING

Let's examine some of the techniques used to control string noise.

It is massively important to be able to silence unwanted string noise—referred to as "muting" the strings. Rock music almost invariably involves distortion (also commonly known as gain or overdrive), which makes it doubly important that your muting is under control. It is a common problem with rock guitar students that they'll get to a certain level where they can play some of their favorite songs, but get increasingly frustrated because even though they're playing all the right shapes, it sounds messy and out of control with all manner of extraneous buzzes, rattles, and excess sounds getting in the way of a clean performance. This is often because they have been so caught up in the various physical hurdles to get to this stage that they forget to actually *listen* to what they are playing, and have failed to realize the absolute necessity of muting correctly.

You are learning rock guitar—not classical, acoustic, country, or jazz—which normally requires playing with distortion, meaning that all the strings on your guitar are more "alive" than using a clean tone. The strings on the guitar produce a certain amount of extraneous noise anyway—but when using distortion this is amplified tenfold so you have to be vigilant at all times in stopping—or "muting"—unwanted strings from ringing and producing sound. This means that the "secret" to playing cool rock guitar is actually being able to control what you *don't* play!

To achieve this, your picking and fretting hands need to work in tandem with each other, not as separate entities. What one hand does needs to be balanced by the other. It will no doubt seem pretty impossible to begin with—you have enough to worry about with each hand individually!—but stick with it: it's very important.

First off let's get the picking hand muting by trying Exercise 1, which is simply playing the note A on the first/top E string. To mute the other strings effectively, make sure that the picking hand is resting on at least the third, fourth, fifth, and sixth strings.

In addition, the tip of your fretting hand's index finger must stub against the second string, thus muting it (see Fig 1). This is an example of both hands working together: the rule is that whichever strings it is impractical for your picking hand to mute, the fretting hand must deal with. This way only the actual string you are playing will be audible, and thus all your playing will be cleaner.

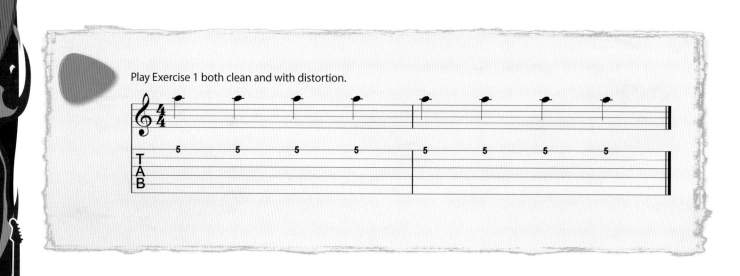

Play Exercise 1 both clean and with distortion.

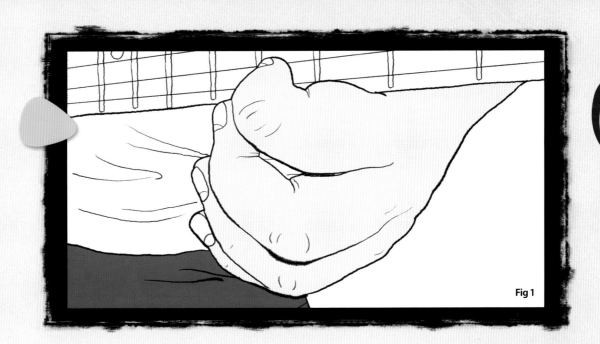

Fig 1

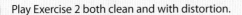

Play Exercise 2 both clean and with distortion.

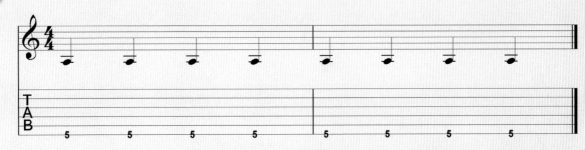

Now let's turn our attention to muting with the fretting hand by looking at Exercise 2, which is again playing the note A, but this time on the sixth/low E string. Not only does your index finger have a requirement to fret the sixth/low E string, but the underside of the index finger must adopt a lazy and relaxed angle across the physically lower strings, gently resting on them with just enough pressure to inhibit them from vibrating, but not so much pressure that you are actually fretting notes (Fig 2).

When you're playing songs and riffs that utilize chords and scales, sometimes in a single phrase, you're going to have to make sure you adjust your hand for whatever it is that you are playing at a particular moment.

Fig 2

PALM MUTING

Palm muting is a component of many famous rock and metal riffs, as well as being vital—with less distortion!—to many other styles of music, particularly funk rhythm. The muting techniques we've so far examined were designed to eliminate unwanted string noise, but picking-hand muting, often called "palm muting," serves as a method of varying (and often intensifying) the tone and attack of what you're playing. For metal guitar this is one area you can't afford to overlook!

Palm muting is based on a simple principle: by positioning the side of your picking hand's palm on the string near the bridge—specifically, just where the string exits the bridge—you alter the tone of the string, eliminating sustain but retaining the inherent quality of the note. By varying the hand's pressure on the string, your hand's angle, and the distance from the bridge where your side of palm contacts the string, you can vary the muted tone produced significantly.

Playing hard and aggressively will really help you generate that infamous metal "chug" much loved of bands such as Black Sabbath, Metallica, Slipknot, and Avenged Sevenfold. Play lighter and you will find it simply tightens up the sound.

In this book most of the muting you will encounter is when you need to have an open sixth/low E string or fifth/A string played as part of a riff. Here are four exercises specifically designed to deal with this.

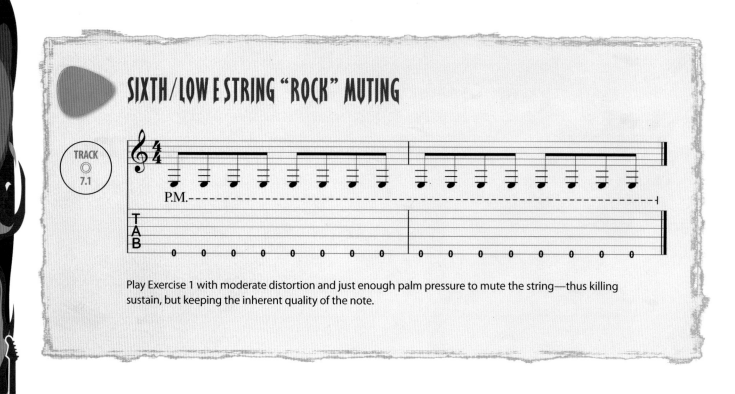

SIXTH/LOW E STRING "ROCK" MUTING

TRACK
7.1

P.M.---

Play Exercise 1 with moderate distortion and just enough palm pressure to mute the string—thus killing sustain, but keeping the inherent quality of the note.

FIFTH/A STRING "ROCK" MUTING

TRACK
○
7.2

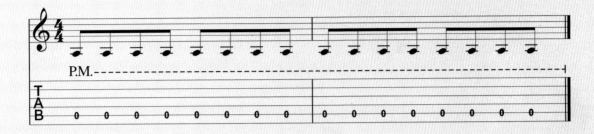

Likewise, Exercise 2 is played with moderate distortion and a lighter touch.

SIXTH/LOW E STRING IN FULL-ON METAL MODE

TRACK
○
7.3

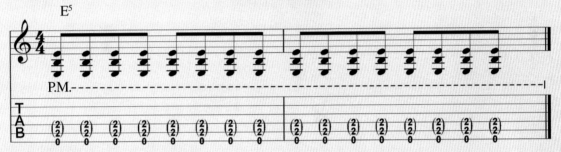

For Exercises 3 and 4, feel free to pile on the gain and dig in hard!

FIFTH/A STRING IN FULL-ON METAL MODE

TRACK
○
7.4

In the last two examples you will note that the fifth/A string and fourth/D strings are fretted at the second fret. Don't worry about this too much—just dig in hard on the picking. These are there to add extra "chug."

Queen, Brian May

CHAPTER THREE:
BASIC TRAINING

Here's where your rock odyssey begins! In this chapter we will be looking at the physical basics of guitar playing: I warn you in advance this isn't going to be the most exciting stuff you'll ever play, but these few pages contain some of the most useful exercises to develop your strength and all-round physical ability that you'll ever encounter. Remember, every journey has to start somewhere.

RHYTHM

Rhythm is the glue that holds music together and these exercises will aid your understanding and ability to play in time.

This is incredibly important, so let's get you acclimatized to both playing and thinking rhythmically and in time. After all, you will at some stage—hopefully pretty soon—be playing with other musicians: if you are all in time with each other it sounds so much better than if you are all thrashing about with your own agendas!

All the exercises in this book are in 4/4. We won't get caught up in explaining time signatures now; just try to tap your foot in time with the tempo and get used to counting 1, 2, 3, 4 with the beat.

WHAT'S TEMPO?

Tempo is the speed of a piece of music measured in beats per minute. The vast majority of exercises in this book are played at 100 bpm—which is a realistic target. However you shouldn't stop there—a lot of songs will require you to play licks either slower or faster and mastering faster licks accurately straight off can be very daunting. The solution to this is to start slowly and gradually build up the tempo using a metronome.

"Old-school" metronome

USING A METRONOME

Practicing with a metronome is a fantastic way of increasing your technical ability, almost without your brain realizing that you are doing so. A lot of obstacles to improving your playing are a result of a mental block: your brain hears something that seems out of reach, then imposes a subconscious barrier that restricts what you are in fact capable of. You are, in effect, fighting yourself—but using a metronome and very gradually increasing the tempo can help conquer this. Once you have mastered a particular exercise at the slow or introductory tempo, increase the speed a click at a time (for non-digital metronomes) or a couple of bpm if using an electronic one. Doing this regularly enables you to increase your speed and technical ability, while maintaining accuracy, without you consciously registering the fact, because the increases in tempo are so negligible. You are, in effect, tricking yourself into reaching targets that initially you might dismiss as unreachable.

In any new practice session—particularly in the early days—you should be able to increase the tempo a couple of clicks/bpm without too much trouble: do this every session and soon enough you will reach your desired tempo. None of the target speeds here are unachievable: regularity and consistency of practice is the key.

It may not feel very rock & roll to be hammering away on your guitar with that annoying click in the background, but believe me, the benefits are massive. At this stage it's all about equipping yourself with the core physical ability to be able to perform music that otherwise would take you ages to achieve.

It is important to realize that all this talk about speed doesn't mean we are training you with the sole objective of being able to play fast—it's just physical training to enable you to perform what is needed to play the songs you want to play without any basic technical restrictions.

Rock, like all musical styles, can vary dramatically in tempo: from a ballad at 70 bpm, a classic rock anthem at around 110 bpm, or a punk rocker at 160 bpm, to a thrash metal speedfest at 200+ bpm.

To tackle some of these is a long way in the distance, but for the purposes of this book, being able to play exercises, melodies, riffs, solos, or licks based around rhythmic groupings of 1, 2, 3, and 4 notes per beat at around 100 bpm should be achievable.

SINGLE-STRING PICKING

For all of these exercises, refer to the single-string picking- and fretting-hand positions sections in Chapter Two. These may be the first exercises you play, but let's start as we mean to go on: be hyper-critical regarding string noise. Clarity over speed rules the day!

In these exercises we are simply going to fret the fifth fret of the first string with the index finger and get used to playing 1, 2, 3, and 4 notes per beat. Then we will introduce what are called rests; and, when each exercise is mastered on the first string, transfer the exercises to the other strings. It's crucial that the only string that is audible is the one you are playing—so, to reiterate, keep aware of your picking and fretting hand positioning—it's all-important! Notice that each of these exercises has a measure where you don't play—and the fact that you don't play a note is shown by those weird-looking little rectangular blocks.

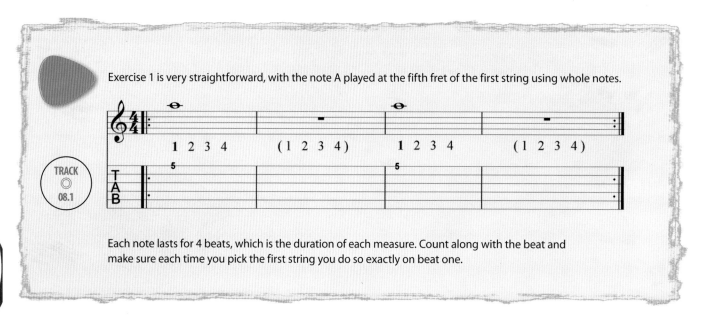

Exercise 1 is very straightforward, with the note A played at the fifth fret of the first string using whole notes.

TRACK
08.1

Each note lasts for 4 beats, which is the duration of each measure. Count along with the beat and make sure each time you pick the first string you do so exactly on beat one.

Having these rest measures is useful because it helps you maintain concentration for a relatively short amount of time, rest, and re-group, then concentrate fully for another four beats, rest, and so on. Also it gets you used to thinking in terms of measures of music and will further engrain the need to keep counting.

This is a crucial point: even now at the beginning of your journey to being a rock hero, try to get used to counting and tapping your foot with the beat for all the exercises and music in this book. Doing this develops your internal "rhythm clock" and helps program your brain and body to gain good basic timekeeping skills.

Incidentally, those double lines with two dots at the beginning and end of each exercise simply mean to repeat that whole section. It's a musical shorthand to save reprinting a section that simply repeats. Get used to these: you will see these signs a lot.

All of these exercises are played at 100 bpm—so once you have mastered this, remember to keep increasing the tempo on the metronome gradually. Refer to the previous page on using the metronome to help you achieve your target tempo.

Anyway, back to work…

Exercise 2 utilizes half notes.

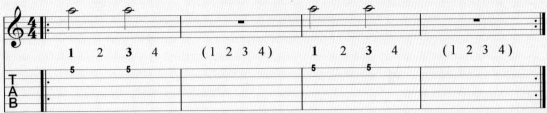

TRACK
08.2

Each note lasts for 2 beats, which means you have to play the string twice in each measure on beat one and beat three. To reiterate: count along with the beat as you play. It is tricky to begin with but you will quickly get used to it…

Exercise 3 introduces quarter notes.

TRACK
08.3

Each note lasts for 1 beat, which means you have to play the string four times in each measure, on beats one, two, three, and four.

Exercise 4 takes us into eighth note territory, which involves alternate picking (see "Let's Alternate" later in this chapter).

TRACK
08.4

Now we have each note lasting for half a beat, which means you have to play the string eight times in each measure. At this point counting really starts to pay dividends, and you need to count 1 and 2 and 3 and 4 and for each measure.

Eighth notes are pretty fundamental to rock guitar—countless riffs and licks are based upon this rhythmic grouping, so get used to it now!

Exercise 5 introduces three notes per beat—known as eighth-note "triplets."

A triplet means that you play 3 notes per beat—so count these as 1&a, 2&a, 3&a, 4&a.

Finally, Exercise 6 looks at sixteenth notes.

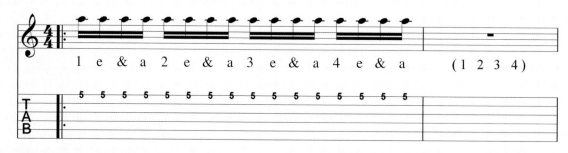

A sixteenth note is basically a way of saying play 4 notes per beat. Lots of metal bands use sixteenths as a basis of riffs, as well as solos: as you will have gathered now it means you play more notes per beats than the previous exercises. Count these as 1e&a, 2e&a, 3e&a, 4e&a.

It is essential that when you've gained a basic ability to play these exercises on the first string, you immediately transfer them to the other strings. Pay particular attention to the muting principles described in Chapter Two: you need to be vigilant in ensuring that the only string that is audible is the one you are performing the exercise on. If you fail to do so, you will encounter "overtones" from the other strings ringing out, which will become particularly apparent when using distortion: another reason to ensure that you practice all the exercises both clean and with distortion.

WEEK
01
DAY 2

RESTS

A "rest" is a musical term that tells you when to silence a note, chord, or phrase. The gaps in music are essential to songs and riffs: when you don't play, and for how long you keep silent are all-important.

To perform a rest, simply mute the desired string. You've already been using whole-note rests in the previous exercises but now let's introduce some shorter rests. Counting is all-important: you will notice that while the counting notation remains constant, the rests are indicated by having the relevant beats shown with brackets. All the previous exercises have dealt with whole-note rests, so there is little point in covering this ground again. Instead let's start with:

HALF-NOTE RESTS

TRACK
09.1

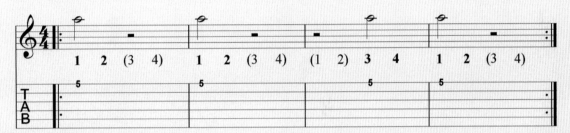

QUARTER-NOTE RESTS

TRACK
09.2

EIGHTH-NOTE RESTS

TRACK
09.3

CHROMATIC PICKING EXERCISES

In previous pages we have looked at the rhythmic aspect of playing single notes: now let's apply those hard-won lessons to more than one note per string, and—crucially—using all your fretting hand's fingers. The purpose of these exercises is not only to augment what you have already learned about rhythm, but also to gain strength, stretch, co-ordination, and flexibility for your fretting hand.

These exercises use all four fingers of your fretting hand, and it should come as no surprise that you will struggle with your pinkie. However, stick with it: treat these as a gym workout for your fingers and practice them daily as your penance to the altar of rock & roll.

As with all the previous exercises, try to perfect these on the first string and then shift to the same patterns to the other ones.

ASCENDING FINGER EXERCISES

Exercise 1 looks at using all four fingers of the fretting hand with an ascending "chromatic" exercise commencing from the fifth fret of the first string. To get you started this is simply quarter notes—i.e., one note per beat.

TRACK
10.1

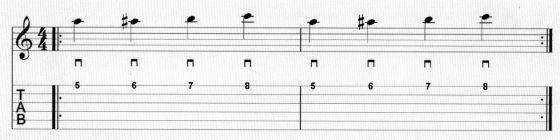

KEEP THOSE FINGERS UNDER CONTROL!

TRACK
10.2

When playing ascending notes on a string leave the "lower fingers" in place once they've fretted their notes, irrespective of how many further notes are still to come.

For example, when you place the second finger down at the sixth fret leave the first one down, when you place the third finger down at the seventh fret, leave both the first and second fingers down, and finally when you place that pesky pinkie down at the eighth fret leave the first, second, and third fingers all in place. This stops excess flailing around, minimizes movement, and encourages a tidy and efficient technique. It's all-important when the time comes to burn that you'll have the necessary physical conditioning to rip it up with ease!

Once you've mastered Exercise 1, transfer to the other strings as shown in Exercise 2 (on the next page).

WHAT DO YOU DO WITH YOUR THUMB?

When playing the first string, the soft pad of your fretting-hand thumb should be hooked over the neck, resting gently on the sixth string—providing a platform for stability. It should roughly be in line with your second finger.

Gradually, as you progress through the strings, your thumb needs to drop down until, by the time you are playing the sixth string, it is balanced in the middle of the back of the neck, akin to the "classical" guitarist's favored position. As you work through the book, try to bear in mind these "rules." The aim is that by being aware of these from day one you will, in time, do them naturally and have developed efficient technique.

MUTE, CONTROL, MUTE, CONTROL...

As we have already noticed, the picking hand not only has to concern itself with generating the note from picking the string, but also to mute the strings physically higher than your target string by resting the heel of the palm on them to stop them ringing. In practice you will find that it can be tricky to deal with the string immediately above the note you are picking, so the tip of your index finger needs to stub against that string, leaving your picking hand to deal with the other strings.

For example, if you are about to play on the second string, the underside of your index finger kills the first string, and the tip stubs against the third string, rendering that one out of action. This leaves the heel/side of your palm—as well as, for some players, the side of your thumb—to control the fourth, fifth, and sixth strings. The bottom line is that the only string that should be audible is the one you are playing: if there is excess noise and it sounds messy, you have forgotten to deal with the muting.

You will notice that we have started these off at the fifth fret, so get comfortable with these, and in the following week try to shift down a fret so you are commencing these from the fourth fret. Take another week, then shift down to the third, and so on. Eventually you should be able to execute these without too much effort.

DESCENDING FINGER EXERCISES

The rules for your picking hand when playing descending notes on a string are the same as when you ascend: your index finger's tip should stub against the next string above to aid muting; your thumb should shift position depending on which string you are playing; and you should have the heel of your hand and/or the side of your picking thumb muting the bass strings. But you don't need to worry about keeping all your fingers down when descending—indeed, it often encourages tension in your hand. Just do what comes naturally.

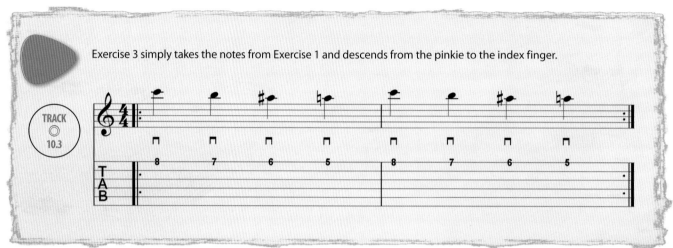

Exercise 3 simply takes the notes from Exercise 1 and descends from the pinkie to the index finger.

TRACK
10.3

Right: Dream Theater's monster guitarist John Petrucci

Exercise 4 transfers this to the other strings.

TRACK
10.4

Finally, Exercise 5 ascends and then descends, covering all six strings.

TRACK
10.5

LET'S ALTERNATE!

Once you are satisfied with your progress in the material we've covered so far, pull it all together into a self-contained workout. This is what I recommend that players of all abilities use as a warm-up; do this as soon as you pick up the guitar, with that ever-present metronome, and you'll find it works wonders.

Notice we are now dealing with eighth notes and this requires "alternate picking."

WHAT'S "ALTERNATE PICKING"?

Alternate picking is simply when you use both the downstrokes/picks (shown as ⊓) that you should be comfortable with by now along with their opposite: upstrokes/picks (shown as V).

WHY USE ALTERNATE PICKING?

The vast majority of new guitarists, if given the chance, will simply down-pick everything they can. Unless you are one of the few who naturally up-pick, down-picking is what comes naturally—and indeed, it is a vital tool that you will use until the end of your days… but it isn't always the best bet.

Think about occasions when you have to pick two consecutive notes on a string—which you will find happens in almost every riff and lick known to humanity! The natural inclination to down-pick is generally the best bet for that first note, but in order to play the second note on that string with a down-pick, you will have (unless you are some sort of higher being blessed with an amazing rotating arm/wrist) to move the pick physically over the string in order to approach that note from above.

So why bother? Just pick that string again with an up-pick—it saves time, minimizes physical movement by 50 percent, and maximizes your efficiency. Which you're going to need to get those hot licks down! The real necessity to use alternate picking arises when you have to play speedier licks and riffs—which, let's face it, as a rock guitarist you will be needing to do!

On the next page is a fully self-contained picking workout that, once mastered on the first/top E string, should be transferred to the other strings.

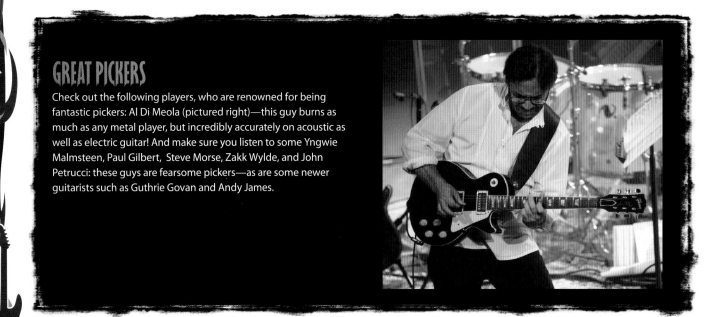

GREAT PICKERS

Check out the following players, who are renowned for being fantastic pickers: Al Di Meola (pictured right)—this guy burns as much as any metal player, but incredibly accurately on acoustic as well as electric guitar! And make sure you listen to some Yngwie Malmsteen, Paul Gilbert, Steve Morse, Zakk Wylde, and John Petrucci: these guys are fearsome pickers—as are some newer guitarists such as Guthrie Govan and Andy James.

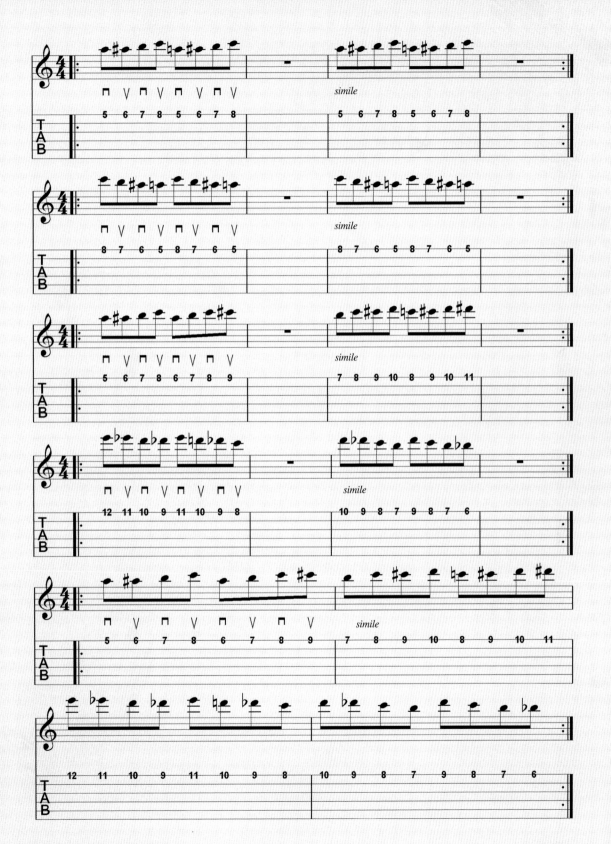

HAMMER-ONS AND PULL-OFFS
"TO PICK OR NOT TO PICK": THAT IS THE QUESTION!

Hammer-ons and pull-offs are when you use your fretting hand's fingers to produce notes rather than the pick.

Exercise 1 shows hammer-ons and pull-offs from between the fifth and seventh frets of the first/top E string.

TRACK
12.1

Before commencing this exercise, make sure that the tip of your first finger is stubbed against the second/B string, and you are resting with the picking hand on the third, fourth, fifth, and sixth strings to mute them.

Hammer-ons and pull-offs work best when played with clarity and precision, and having lots of extraneous string noise rather ruins the effect! The basic problem is getting enough muscle power from your finger to sound the note. You need to treat each finger as a sort of hammer—as if you are trying to push the string into the fretboard in a similar manner to hammering a nail into a plank of wood. You need to get enough height from the string to enable you to harness physical momentum. A limp placement of your finger on the string will not work, so beef it up!

A pull-off is a hammer-on in reverse. If you are fretting the seventh fret of the first/top E string (the note B), have your first finger in place fretting the fifth note of the same string (the note A). Pick that seventh fret, then pull your third finger down, performing a sort of fretting-hand plucking motion. This momentum will then

make the fifth fret sound clearly without the need to pick it. At this stage, don't simply lift your finger off in an upward motion—you need that downward motion to generate enough volume on the lower note.

Due to the physical characteristics of the guitar neck, hammer-ons are designed for playing higher notes from lower notes. Pull-offs are for producing lower notes from higher notes.

Hammer-ons and pull-offs result in a smoother sound, as the "click" sound that a pick generates when you pick a note is now absent and is, as you will later see, integral to many of the most famous licks and riffs in rock history.

You will also find that for speedier passages it's often a lot easier, as you don't have to worry about your picking as much, although your picking hand still has to retain all its muting duties.

When used together, hammer-ons and pull-offs are often referred to as legato—an Italian term used in standard music notation to mean "smoothly."

Exercise 2 looks at using the second, first, and third and fourth fingers to hammer on from the first finger.

TRACK
12.2

Exercise 3 looks at pulling off from the second, third, and fourth fingers to the first finger.

TRACK
12.3

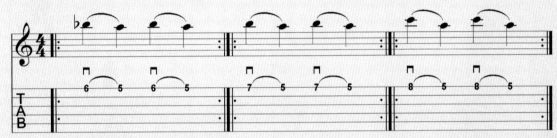

You will probably find that it is easiest using the third finger, and hardest with that poor old pinkie: this is normal and to be expected so don't panic! Just persevere and it will come.

Exercise 4 looks at combining hammer-ons and pull-offs.

TRACK
12.4

Exercise 5 looks at hammering on consecutive notes.

TRACK
◎
12.5

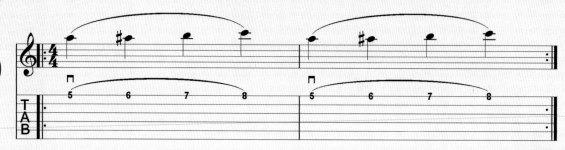

Exercise 6 looks at pulling off consecutive notes.

TRACK
◎
12.6

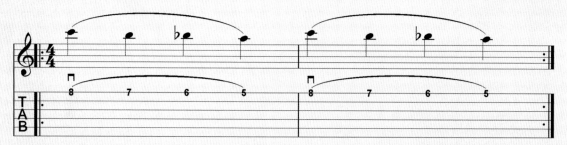

Exercise 7 looks at hammering on consecutive notes ascending the neck and then using pull-offs to descend again. This exercise should be familiar to you as it is a legato version of the final exercise from your alternate picking workout.

TRACK
◎
12.7

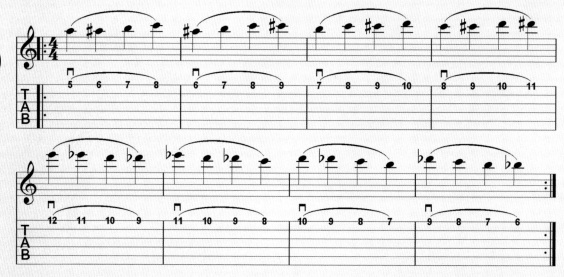

Exercise 8 applies the same chromatic principle that we've already encountered and uses consecutive hammer-ons and pull-offs: these are sometimes referred to as legato rolls.

To conclude, make sure you transfer these exercises to all the other strings in the now familiar process of nailing them on the first string, shifting to the second string, then the third, and so on.

Don't just jump in on the sixth string—it's considerably harder due to your fretting hand having to deal with the mass of the neck, and is best tackled when you have more playing time and experience under your belt.

THE SMOOTHEST OF THE SMOOTH

Check out the following players who are renowned for being supreme legato players: Allan Holdsworth—the ultimate guitarist's guitarist for advanced legato playing. And make sure you listen to some Eddie Van Halen, Joe Satriani (pictured right), Steve Vai, and Brett Garsed.

OPEN POWER CHORD EXERCISES

Well done! You've dealt with the single-string exercises—which means that you should be set up well for when we deal with scales and scale-derived riffs and licks. However, by far the biggest percentage of your playing time will be devoted to playing rhythm guitar, which in rock and metal mainly consists of power chords.

WHAT'S A POWER CHORD?

The power chord—or "fifth"—is basically a simplified version of a "normal" chord such as a major or minor. These first became widely used when distortion was adopted by guitarists as a tone of choice back in the 1960s: many players found that playing conventional chords with this newfangled "rock sound" sounded messy.

A simplified version that maintained the basic melodic function of the original chord (for example an A major still sounded suitably "A-ish") but sounded tighter and more defined when using distortion was thus required. Gradually players realized that by changing the fingerings and getting rid of one of the notes (see

Chapter Nine if you want to know the theory), they created a two-note variation that, when played through an amp set on stun, wowed the listener with its powerful sound: thus the power chord was born.

The following exercises all use the most common "open" power chords: A5, D5, and E5. You will notice that one of the notes is bracketed: that is because it is the same as the root note, merely an octave higher. This means that it's not essential to play—it depends on the situation you find yourself in at any given time, as its main function is to thicken up the sound. Use your ears to decide…

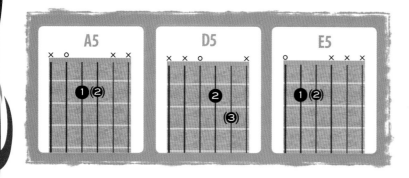

Exercise 1 looks at playing A5 to D5 to E5 using whole notes.

TRACK
13.1

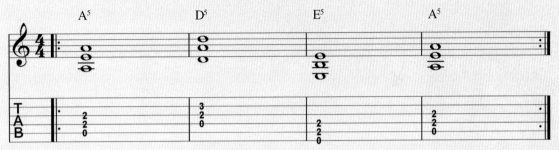

Exercise 2 looks at playing A5 to D5 to E5 using quarter notes.

TRACK
13.2

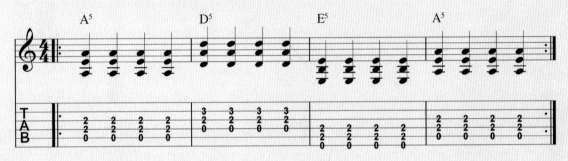

Exercise 3 looks at playing A5 to D5 to E5 using eighth notes.

TRACK
13.3

TRACK
13.4

Exercise 4 looks at playing A5 to D5 to E5 using quarter notes and inserting quarter-note rests.

TRACK
13.5

Exercise 5 looks at playing A5 to D5 to E5 using eighth notes and inserting eighth-note rests.

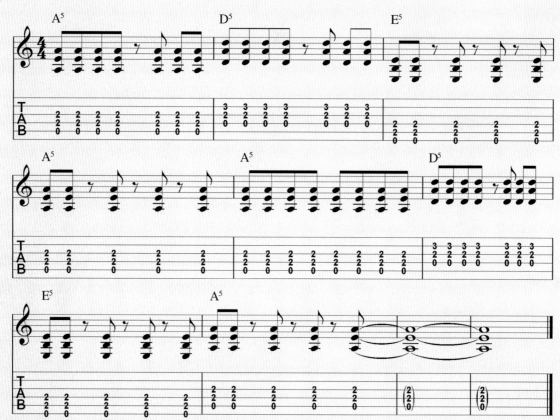

MOVEABLE POWER CHORDS

Now we are moving into using moveable shapes. You'll be pleased to know that these are a real bonus for ease of learning: basically once you've got a chord or scale "shape" under your fingers, that shape is transferrable both up and down the neck.

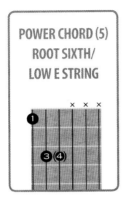

POWER CHORD (5)
ROOT SIXTH/
LOW E STRING

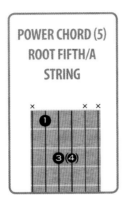

POWER CHORD (5)
ROOT FIFTH/A
STRING

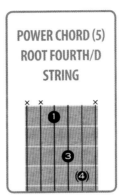

POWER CHORD (5)
ROOT FOURTH/D
STRING

You can play any power chord using one of the above shapes—which one you choose to use depends upon the musical situation you may find yourself in: for example, the root sixth shapes tend to have the most heaviness or "depth," because of the thickness of the strings. The root fourth, being constructed off thinner strings, arguably tends to have more clarity. As an exercise, try to play G5 using each of the above shapes. To do this, you need to locate the note G on the sixth, fifth, and fourth strings, and simply play the above shapes from the frets where G is located—refer to "The Notes on the Fretboard" in Chapter One. If you are successful, you will have played the power chord root sixth from the third fret, the power chord root fifth from the tenth fret, and the power chord root fourth from the fifth fret.

You should find that the shapes are fairly easy to play; just make sure that the index finger is muting the strings marked "X." Now try the following exercises.

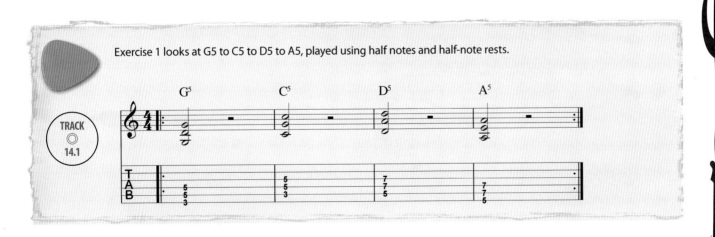

Exercise 1 looks at G5 to C5 to D5 to A5, played using half notes and half-note rests.

TRACK
14.1

Exercise 2 looks at quarter notes.

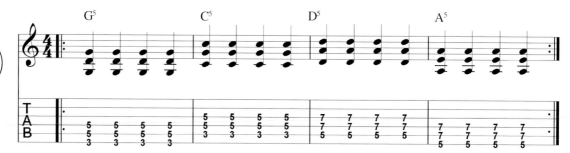

Exercise 3 looks at playing these in straight eighth notes.

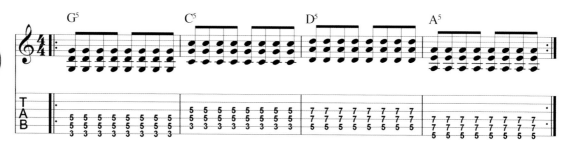

Finally, Exercise 4 puts in a couple of rests.

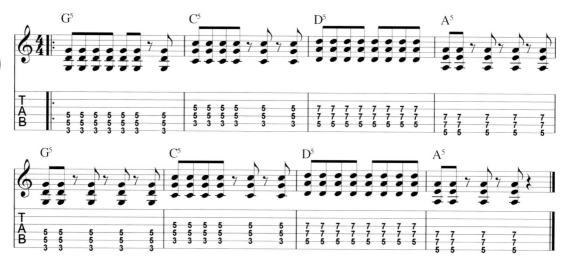

That should do it for now: get super-comfortable with these and you'll be ready for the riffs in Chapter Four.

OPEN CHORDS

So far we've looked at single-note and power chord exercises that are primarily designed to be used with distortion; however, the sound of a clean guitar or acoustic has driven thousands of rock songs over the years, most often playing standard "open chords," so we need to get you up to speed on this super-quick!

WHAT'S AN OPEN CHORD?

An open chord is simply a chord that utilizes "open" (i.e., non-fretted) strings. Try the following chords: these are all played on the CD so you can check that you are playing them correctly. A good exercise would be to practice changing randomly between these chords.

A major
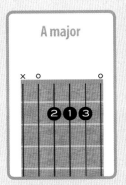

A minor
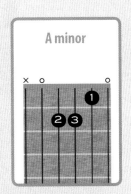

A7
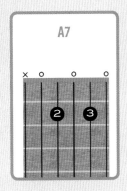

Asus2
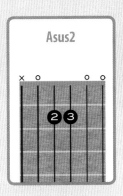

Asus4
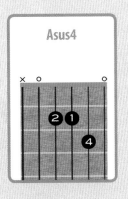

C major
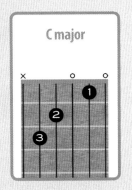

Cmaj7
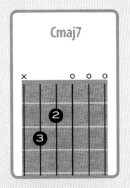

Cadd9
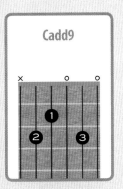

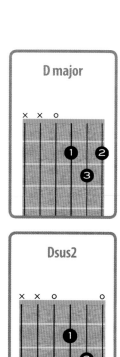

D major

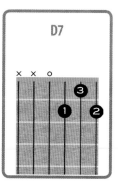

D minor

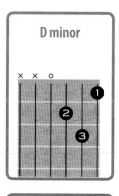

D7

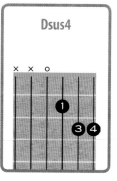

Dsus4

Dsus2

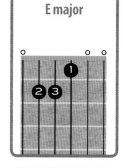

E major

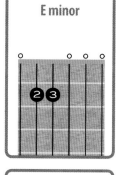

E minor

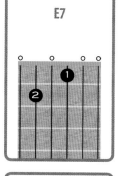

E7

Esus4

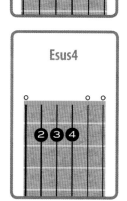

Fmaj7

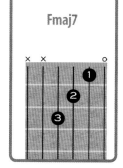

G major

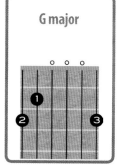

"Big" G major

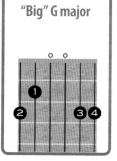

An effective method in both finger and memory training is to take any two chords from the above and practice switching between them repeatedly. For example:

A to D x 20

D to E x 20

E to G x 20

Then progress onto any other two chords at random: it doesn't matter which two chords you choose, the importance is in the repetition of movement as this builds up "muscle memory." You don't even have to utilize the picking hand—switching between the chord shapes will be enough to "hard wire" the basic shapes and physical movements into your brain so that when the time comes to put the chords into practice with a "real" song, all you have to concentrate on are the dynamics of the song or riff involved.

OPEN CHORD EXERCISES

These exercises all utilize the following chords:

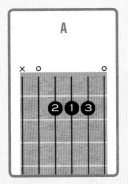
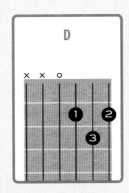
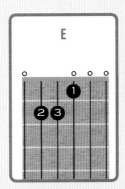

Exercise 1 looks at playing A to D to E in basic quarter notes.

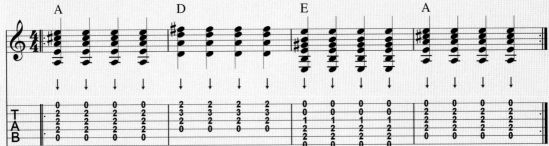

You will notice that the downward arrows have replaced the down-pick shapes we encountered in the single-string exercises. This emphasizes the difference between "strumming" (which covers several strings) and "picking" (which covers a single string at a time).

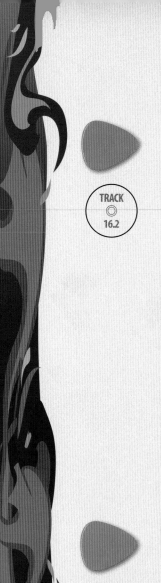

Exercise 2 looks at playing A to D to E in basic quarter notes with quarter-note rests.

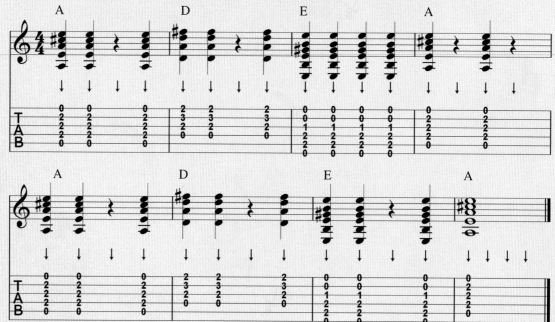

Exercise 3 looks at the same three chords but using eighth notes. You will note that for the off beats (the "&" of each beat) it is common practice to use an upward strum.

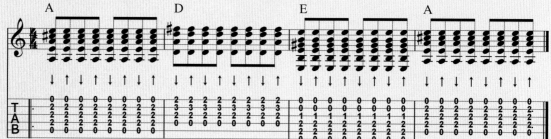

Exercise 4 looks at playing this now very familiar pattern but picking out each string at a time. It is beneficial to get comfortable with this now because it not only helps you clearly hear each string (and thus deal with any that are not ringing clearly by adjusting the fretting hand angle) but also to introduce you to "arpeggios."

TRACK
16.4

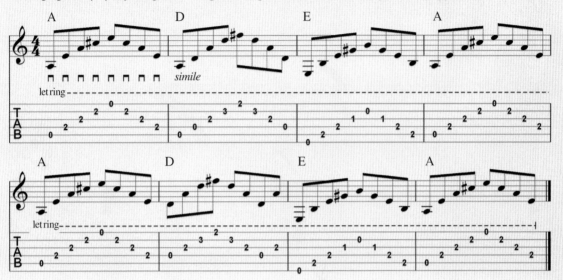

Exercise 5 looks at playing A, D, and E chords with eighth notes and eighth rests.

TRACK
16.5

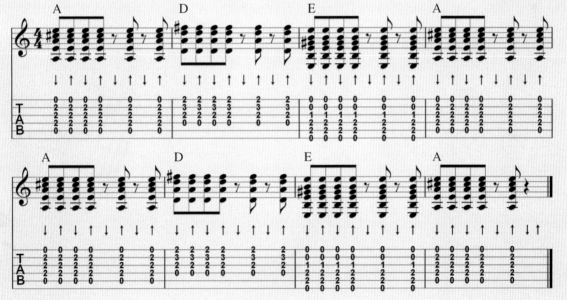

BARRE CHORD EXERCISES

Now we turn our attention to barre chords: these can be viewed as the more expansive cousins to the power chords you are already familiar with. A barre chord is a moveable chord shape that uses your index finger to "bar" several strings at a time. There are loads of barre chords in common use, but for this book you need concern yourself only with root sixth and fifth string major, minor, and dominant seventh chords.

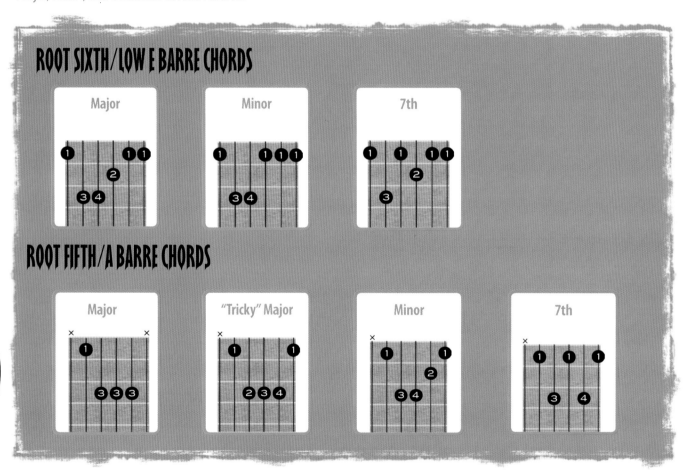

ROOT SIXTH/LOW E BARRE CHORDS

Major — Minor — 7th

ROOT FIFTH/A BARRE CHORDS

Major — "Tricky" Major — Minor — 7th

TECHNICAL NOTES

Try all these examples, picking out each string individually so you can hear any strings that are not being fretted properly. A lot of these require subtly different finger and hand placement in order to gain clarity: you will probably find that with the root sixth string minor shapes the third string needs attention; and the root fifth major shape is a consistent pain to get your third finger to fret all three strings accurately.

Exercise 1 looks at playing Am to F to G in strummed quarter notes with rests using sixth string shapes.

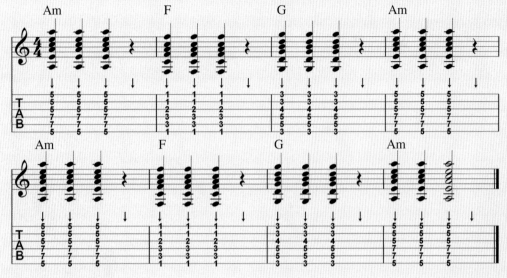

Exercise 2 looks at playing Am to F to G in strummed eighth notes using root sixth string shapes.

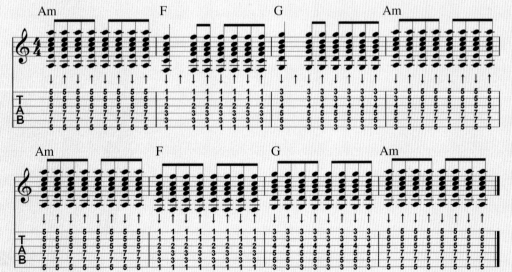

Exercise 3 looks at playing Em to C to D in quarter notes using root fifth string shapes.

TRACK
17.3

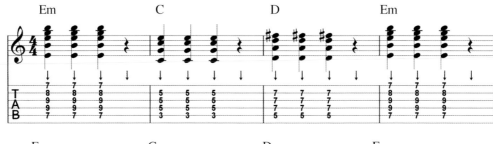

Exercise 4 looks at the same thing, only using eighth notes.

TRACK
17.4

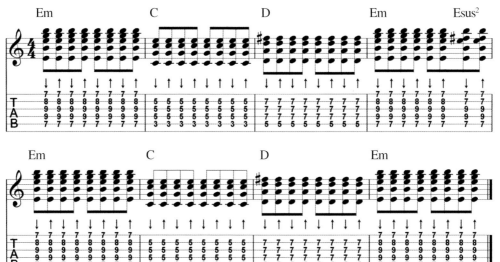

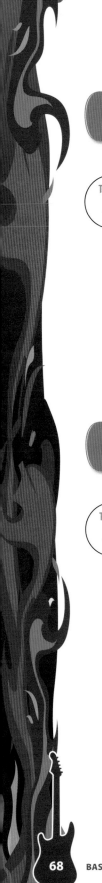

Exercise 5 mixes root sixth and fifth string barre chords.

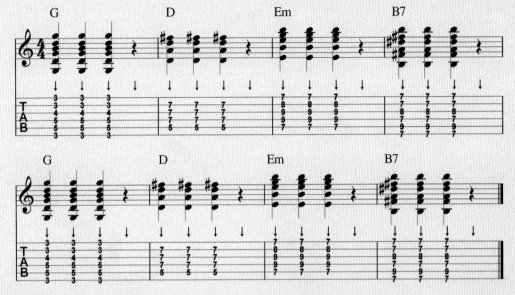

Finally, let's try the same chords in eighth notes.

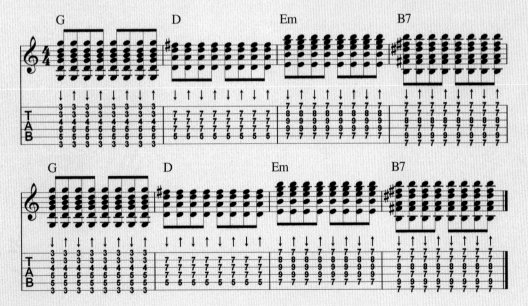

CHAPTER FOUR:
OPEN CHORD RIFFS

After slogging your way through all the technique exercises in the previous chapter, now comes the time to put it all into practice and make some "real" music. In this chapter we're looking at riffs in the style of some rock classics that have been arranged specifically around some basic open chords—so get ready to rock!

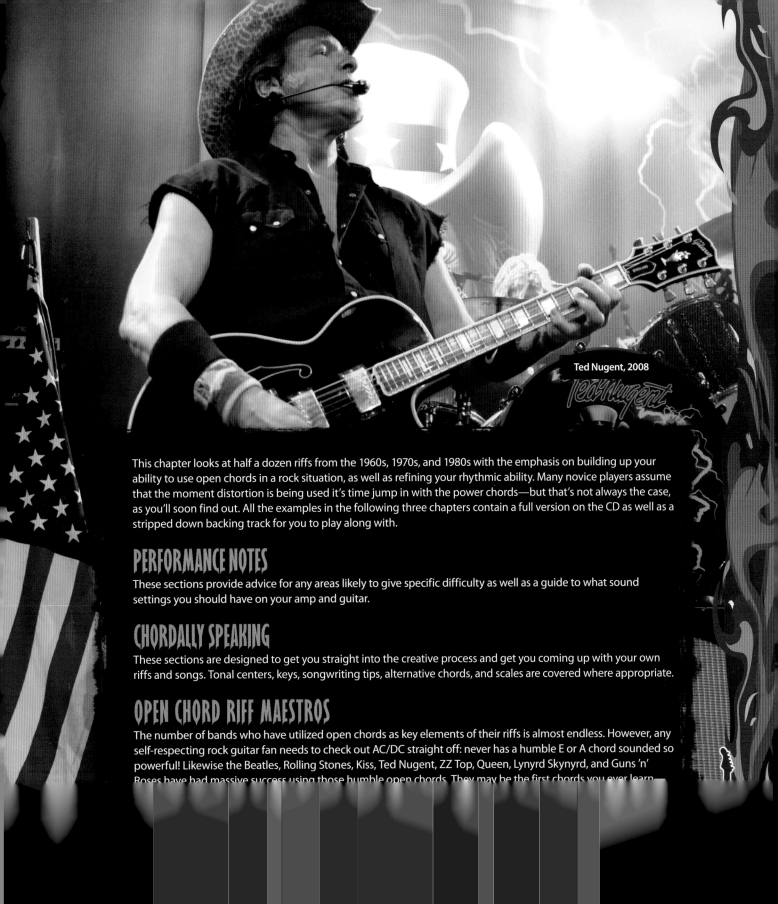

Ted Nugent, 2008

This chapter looks at half a dozen riffs from the 1960s, 1970s, and 1980s with the emphasis on building up your ability to use open chords in a rock situation, as well as refining your rhythmic ability. Many novice players assume that the moment distortion is being used it's time jump in with the power chords—but that's not always the case, as you'll soon find out. All the examples in the following three chapters contain a full version on the CD as well as a stripped down backing track for you to play along with.

PERFORMANCE NOTES

These sections provide advice for any areas likely to give specific difficulty as well as a guide to what sound settings you should have on your amp and guitar.

CHORDALLY SPEAKING

These sections are designed to get you straight into the creative process and get you coming up with your own riffs and songs. Tonal centers, keys, songwriting tips, alternative chords, and scales are covered where appropriate.

OPEN CHORD RIFF MAESTROS

The number of bands who have utilized open chords as key elements of their riffs is almost endless. However, any self-respecting rock guitar fan needs to check out AC/DC straight off: never has a humble E or A chord sounded so powerful! Likewise the Beatles, Rolling Stones, Kiss, Ted Nugent, ZZ Top, Queen, Lynyrd Skynyrd, and Guns 'n' Roses have had massive success using those humble open chords. They may be the first chords you ever learn—

"ALL RIGHT PAUL?"

British Blues rockers Free originally released "All Right Now" in 1970 and the song has been an international hit on a number of occasions over the years: it contains one of the most famous, best loved, and instantly recognizable riffs in rock history!

"All Right Now" is actually deceptively tricky to play correctly—so here we've stripped the song down to absolute basics. "All Right Paul?" (affectionately named after Free's late great guitarist Paul Kossof) just uses A, D, and G chords. That's it! But, as you'll see, by playing them in a similar rhythm and style you'll be able to knock out your own version with ease!

PERFORMANCE NOTES

This is a prime example of using space in a riff—the rests are as important as the chords here, so make sure you really nail them. Ensure that you're on the bridge pickup, your guitar volume pot is maxed out, and you have a moderate gain—enough to give this some crunch, but not too much or it will sound mushy and too "metal." You want to be able to hear the individual strings, but also have just enough dirt to make it rock!

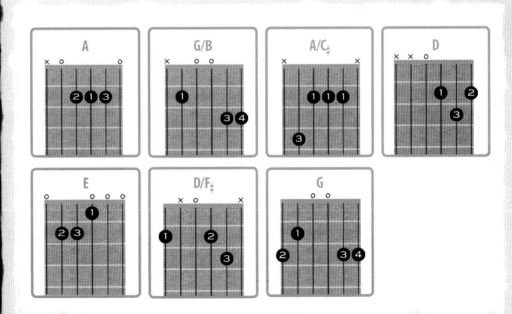

CHORDALLY SPEAKING

The tonal center of this track is A, but as this features a G major chord we're not specifically in the key of A (see Chapter Nine for a list of the "correct" chords in the key of A.) Thus, we've included some other chords for you to experiment with that aren't necessarily tied together theoretically, but which, in practice, fit well together for this style of music.

Try making up some riffs by mixing up the following chords in any order or rhythm you can think of, experiment, and above all else, have fun!

"MAD THING"

"Mad Thing" is a riff in the style of "Wild Thing" and is another great example of a three-chord classic—it's dead easy to play and instantly recognizable.

Troggs, 1960

Released by 1960s rockers The Troggs, this song topped the charts in the US in 1966, has been covered numerous times, and remains an enduring staple of many bands' live set.

For this example we are simply using the chords A, D, and E—so listen to the CD and get ready to play along!

PERFORMANCE NOTES

This is a great example of the simplest of chord progressions being played with a cool, distinctive rhythm and pronounced rests. Result? An iconic riff that helped lay the foundations for many riffs since that have become famous in their own right.

Go for a moderately overdriven tone, and make sure you play with attitude—no wimpy indie strumming here folks! Use your bridge pickup and keep volume on 10 all the way.

Once you've got this riff down, experiment making up your own by changing the rhythm, or order of chords—or whatever! Once you've exhausted A, D, and E, introduce some of the other chords shown opposite. Have fun!

♩ = 100

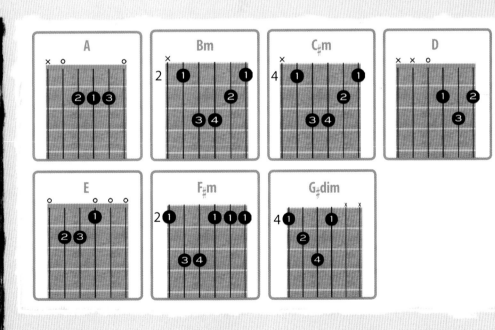

CHORDALLY SPEAKING

The tonal center here is A, but unlike "All Right Paul?" all three chords actually belong to the key of A too—so no tweaking here, just standard chords in the key of A for you to practice.

Integrating minor chords can be hard at first, and G# dim can be a nightmare! Keep at it though—a lot of songs use both major and minor chords. Diminished chords are less common in rock and metal, so feel free to ignore that one!

A

Bm

C#m

D

E

F#m

G#dim

"HEY JIMI"

Legendary guitarist Jimi Hendrix scored his first chart success with "Hey Joe" in 1966.

Jimi Hendrix, 1969

"Hey Jimi" is a simplified version using the basic open chords of C, G, D, A, and E. The original version uses more advanced forms of these same basic chords with loads of Jimi's great chordal embellishments. This back-to-basics version is a great exercise in introducing those "bigger stretch" C and G chords into your vocabulary to the A, D, and E chords we've already encountered.

PERFORMANCE NOTES

Notice that on the E chord we add variation by playing the E, A, and D strings open to maintain interest and provide a cool riff. This works equally as well with either a fully clean amp tone, or a mildly distorted one. If using some distortion, you may want to experiment by backing off on the guitar's volume pot. Doing so shouldn't actually decrease the volume produced (unless you are using a real budget basement amp) but will "clean up" the sound so you can retain individual string clarity. Notice that on the E chords there are several times when the fourth and fifth strings are played "open" to provide variation and retain interest: this device can be referred to as a "fill."

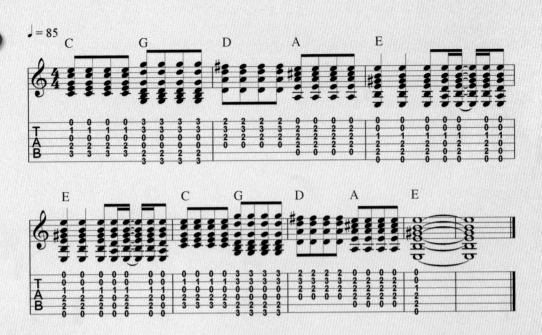

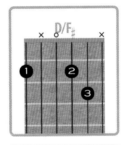

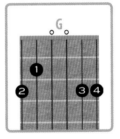

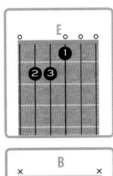

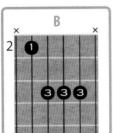

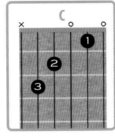

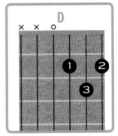

"SWEET OLD ALABAMA"

Southern rockers Lynyrd Skynyrd recorded "Sweet Home Alabama" as a rousing if ironic celebration of the American South, and this redneck classic has endured as one of the best loved feel-good songs in history.

Lynyrd Skynyrd, Gary Rossington

A massive international hit several times over the past 35 years—as well as being a favorite for advertisers across the world—this song has yet again seen renewed success on the back of Kid Rock's homage to the song with his worldwide smash hit single "All Summer Long."

PERFORMANCE NOTES

The original version is considerably trickier to play than "Sweet Old Alabama." Here we've stripped it down to its core basics. Notice the introduction of a variation of C—the Cadd9—and an open G5. These two chords sit well together from a physical playing perspective, as they share many notes. You will note that the third and fourth fingers remain in the same place. Indeed, the third finger has a real easy ride on this piece—it just sits on that third fret B string (the note D) for the duration of the riff. Tonally, this works equally well with a clean tone or a mildly overdriven one—just remember to knock a bit of volume off from the guitar volume pot. Having a bit of dirt in there helps "warm" the sound up and make it sound less clinical.

CHORDALLY SPEAKING

Another new tonal center with D and the featured chords here include a couple of interesting choices: an open G5 "power chord" instead of the standard G (sounds great with a bit of dirt!) and a Cadd9 in place of the normal C to aid both melodic continuity and ease of fingering. Again, have a crack at some of your own riffs.

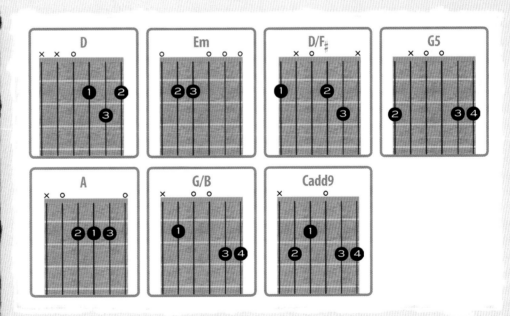

"BACK TO BLACK"

AC/DC's *Back In Black* is the second-biggest-selling album in history—and its title track must be *the* prime candidate for the "Best Riff Ever" award!

AC/DC, Angus Young

Aussie rockers AC/DC have been raising hell since 1974 and by the turn of the decade were firmly established as one of hard rock's finest live bands. After tragedy struck when Bon Scott died, the band regrouped with Geordie vocalist Brian "Beano" Johnson at the helm (as well as super producer Robert "Mutt" Lange) and unleashed the titanic *Back In Black* in 1980.

Almost three decades later, in November 2008 AC/DC achieved the remarkable feat of selling 10 million records in one month—5 million from new album *Black Ice* and 5 million from the back catalog on top.

PERFORMANCE NOTES

"Back To Black" is a simplified version of the original version—we've basically just added a G5 in place of those cool single-note fills. This version nevertheless conjures up the spirit of the original and is a great example of using space. Get some decent overdrive in on this one, but not too much. Listen to the original and you will note that Malcolm Young's tone is actually much cleaner than you might think.

CHORDALLY SPEAKING

Back to E again—you know the drill by now: experiment with your own riffs, based upon the following chords.

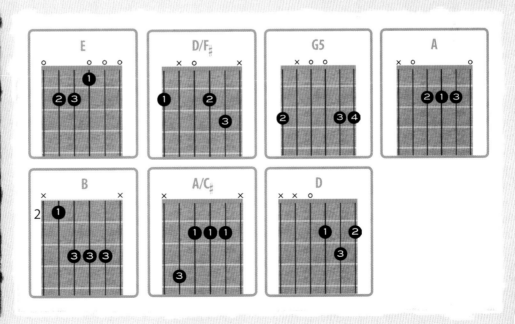

"SWEET CHILD OF ROSES"

Guns 'n' Roses exploded onto the rock scene in 1987 with what would become the decade's best-selling debut album, *Appetite for Destruction*, which featured hits aplenty, including "Paradise City" and "Welcome To The Jungle."

Slash

We're going to take a look at an easy-to-master riff based on the epic "Sweet Child Of Mine." This song will always be synonymous with lead guitarist Slash's famous Gibson Les Paul-conducted creamy arpeggio-based melody—yet it also features a punchy chorus that turns on the attitude after those romantic verses.

PERFORMANCE NOTES

Nice and straightforward this one—but note that we are using a root fifth/A string major barre chord shape in place of a standard open C. Doing so helps tighten up the sound as we are attacking quite hard and tight with this one. You may also notice that we have a Dsus4 adding melodic interest in measures 3 and 4.

Try to make sure this one "swings" and you don't play it too "straight"—think "groove" not "metal"… Again, experiment with the amount of muting you need.

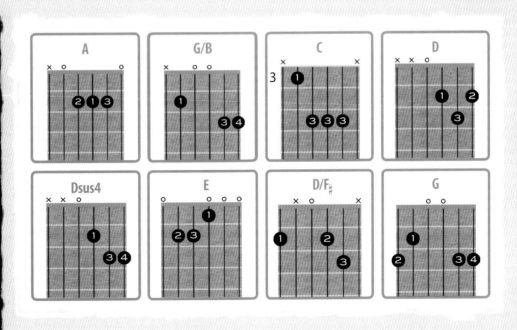

CHORDALLY SPEAKING

To conclude, we're back to to the start, with a tonal center of A, but notice that, again, we're varying the accompanying chord choices. The D sus4 is a hugely popular chord for guitarists—physically, it's very easy to play and it's supremely versatile too, not only as an accompaniment to D but also as a transition device to progress smoothly to many other chords.

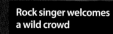
Rock singer welcomes a wild crowd

CHAPTER FIVE:
FEEL THE POWER

Having worked your way from the 1960s to the 1980s using open chords in the previous chapter, it's time to start cranking up the gain with some heavy-duty riffs that feature rock and metal's best buddy: the "power chord"!

Fans reach for
the rock god

Since power chords first came to prominence in the 1960s, they have come to dominate rock and metal songwriting and riffs. In this chapter we examine the use of power chords with ten riff studies from the 1960s through to the present day. Some of these also include power chord variations that have become popular, as well as some cool "triad" shapes (think 3 note power chords) that bands such as AC/DC and Van Halen have used to great effect. As a lot of these riffs are dependant upon a hefty amount of distortion you are going to have to be vigilant in your string control—so all those muting exercises you worked through in Chapter Three are going to be a great help in attaining an accurate performance. All the examples in this chapter contain a full version on the CD as well as a stripped down backing track for you to play along with.

PERFORMANCE NOTES

These sections provide advice for areas likely to give difficulty, as well as a guide to the sound settings for your amp and guitar.

POWER PICKS AND TRIADIC TIPS

These sections are designed to get you straight into the creative process and get you coming up with your own riffs and songs. Tonal centers, keys, song writing tips, alternative chords, and scales are covered where appropriate.

POWER CHORD HEROES AND TRIADIC TRAILBLAZERS

Power chords and triads are the very lifeblood of rock and metal—think of any successful band in this genre and you'll find that 5ths are a feature of almost every song they've ever released: however a few pioneers need consideration. The holy trinity of Led Zeppelin, Black Sabbath, and Deep Purple are absolutely vital listening, as are Iron Maiden and Metallica. Black Sabbath's riffmeister general Tony Iommi absolutely wrote the book on making the power chord the force it is today. Triads tend to be avoided by the heaviest bands as the massive distortion they use renders them ineffective, but Eddie Van Halen's use of these

"WANT TO BE WILD"

"Born To Be Wild" is a cast-iron biker classic by 1960s rockers Steppenwolf, and features a real piledriver of a riff. A favorite with bar bands all over the world, this one is always guaranteed to bring the house down!

Steppenwolf

"Want To Be Wild" takes the basic rhythmic qualities of the famous opening riff, but omits some of the larger stretches of the original, substituting some easier power chords. Make sure you check out the original as it's one of those important riffs that all rock guitarists should know: when you're more experienced, make sure you give it a go—but in the meantime this should do just fine!

PERFORMANCE NOTES

Aim for a relaxed fretting hand: you almost need to "bounce" off the power chords—but don't let your fingers totally lose contact as they need to mute the fifth/A and fourth/D strings so that the chug of the sixth/low E string provides a great contrast to the crunch of the power chords.

Equally, that pronounced bouncing motion should be adopted by your picking hand: on this sort of riff it's sheer energy and motion—rather than perfect clinical execution—that you're after.

It is worth experimenting with how much you mute the sixth/low E string open notes: here I have adopted a medium approach—not so hard that it sounds too "metal," but just enough to add clarity and aid note separation.

Go for a decently overdriven tone, and make sure you play with some real deal "attitude"—use your bridge pickup and keep the volume on 10 all the way…

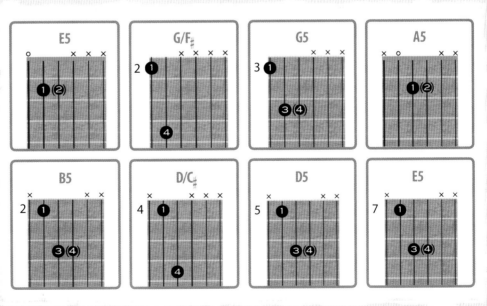

TRACK
32+33

"WHOLE LOTTA LED"

Led Zeppelin's reputation as the ultimate 1970s supergroup remains to this day—and their success is equally legendary: after The Beatles, Led Zeppelin are the biggest selling rock band in history.

Led Zeppelin, L–R:
Robert Plant, Jimmy Page

The original "Whole Lotta Love" features a tight and driving riff that alternates between two single notes and a power chord, with yet again that sixth/low E string pounding away to create an iconic and driving riff. You'll soon realize that many riffs share the same basic components: it's what you with do them that counts! Released in 1968, and the lead track from Led Zeppelin's second album, this is a justifiably world-famous and influential riff!

PERFORMANCE NOTES

The performance considerations from "Want To Be Wild" remain valid here, apart from the fact that we have some single notes to deal with as well. It is especially important to emphasize the clear distinction between the power chords and the single-string melody notes here. Your fretting hand will need to be close in and controlled for the single notes, before relaxing its position to strike the power chords with sufficient energy.

An often-underrated aspect of Zeppelin's work was an innate sense of groove—try to make sure this one swings a bit and you don't play it too straight.

Again, experiment with the amount of muting you need to apply to the low E open-string notes: too much is too metal; too little and you risk the strings bleeding into the power chords. It's another trial and error situation here folks… but great for getting you to familiarize yourself with this instrument we love so much!

Up the overdrive a bit here, and again play with attitude. Use your bridge pickup and keep volume on 10 all the way.

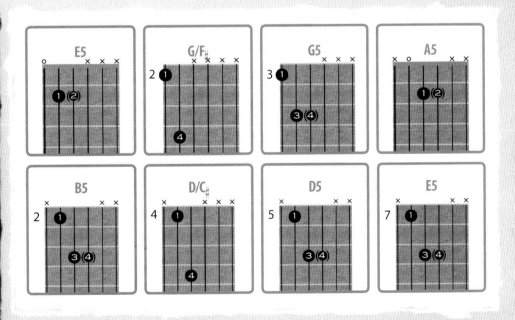

POWER PICKS

Like the previous riff, "Whole Lotta Led" is in E and, due to its similarly driving sound, it's best to use the same basic collection of power chords to start with.

However, this time when you're experimenting try and interject some single note riffs in between those power chords: don't worry about what the actual notes are—just play around until something grabs your attention. You just might come up with something that one day we'll be reading about and learning!

"SABBATH MAN"

Often described as the first true example of heavy metal, Black Sabbath emerged at the tail end of the 1960s with a unique blend of power, mystique, and sheer heaviness that has proved to be immensely influential.

Black Sabbath, L–R: (back) Geezer Butler, Tony Iommi, (front) Bill Ward, Ozzy Osbourne

"Iron Man" is a key track from Sabbath's second album *Paranoid*, released in 1970. In their original guise the band featured Ozzy Osbourne on vocals, but it is to guitarist Tony Iommi that every metal band in the world owes an unmatched debt. This guy wrote the rulebook on metal guitar riffing—Tony, we salute you!

PERFORMANCE NOTES

A great exercise in getting fluent at playing power chords and shifting them around the neck, this is relatively straightforward to play, as all power chords are based on the fifth/A string. However, the shifts are large in places, and fairly speedy—so practice slowly and get the basic moves under your fingers. The main area to watch from a physical perspective is the slides between the G5 and F#5 power chords—make sure you retain adequate finger pressure to keep the notes intact but don't squeeze so hard that your hand locks up, or you wont be able to attain those fluid shifts.

Pump up that overdrive more than the riffs we've so far looked at—but make sure you hold enough back for later on when we really hit the metal!

POWER PICKS

Black Sabbath are renowned for their gloomy minor key-based songs, and "Sabbath Man" is the first example we've looked at so far that possesses a truly definable "minor" quality. Compositionally this is very straightforward: power chords constructed from each note of the B minor scale (B, C#, D, E, F#, G, A) so if you want to try your hand at a dark riff, use these as a starting point.

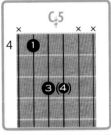

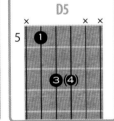

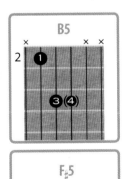

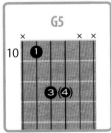

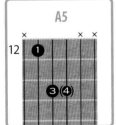

"SMOKIN' ALL NIGHT LONG"

Now you're getting comfortable with power chords, let's turn our attention to fourths (also often referred to as "double stops") and look at a riff inspired by a couple of inspirational songs from the great Ritchie Blackmore.

Deep Purple, Ritchie Blackmore, 1974

The first needs no introduction really. Deep Purple's 1972 song "Smoke On The Water" contains arguably the most famous riff in rock history, and shares a lot of characteristics that most other iconic riffs possess: it's catchy as hell and pretty damn easy to play!

After Ritchie left Deep Purple in 1975 he formed Rainbow, who also enjoyed worldwide success, until Ritchie got back together with Purple in 1984. Here we've taken inspiration from Rainbow's 1978 track "All Night Long" and mixed it up with a little bit of "Smoke On The Water" —the result is this little ditty in front of you now!

You will note that there's not a standard power chord in sight—so also treat this as an exercise in developing your ability to use fourths: they are essential and very cool riff and lick tools—just ask ZZ Top's Billy Gibbons…

PERFORMANCE NOTES

Execute these fourths with one finger— flatten the tip more than is required with power chords so both strings ring true. Use your first finger for the third frets, and your third finger for the fifth and sixth. Don't take the easy option of using separate fingers for each string as in the long run you'll regret it. Ritchie is famed for the uniquely thick tone he got out of his Fender Strats—your best bet is to max the volume and use the bridge pickup, although if you've got a budget Strat copy you could try the neck pickup. Make sure you use a decent amount of overdrive.

SCALEWISE

"Smokin' All Night Long" has a tonal center of G, and its pretty heavily defined minor feel would normally suggest playing around with the key of G minor. But here we're not really dealing with specific chords, power chords, or even scales—more a collection of fourths between the third and the sixth frets that sound cool—so all bets are off. Have a go with the accompanying fourths, experiment, and see what you come up with.

"BAD COMPANY WITH ANGUS"

Bad Company rose from the ashes of Free and achieved massive success in the US in the early to mid 1970s—just as some upstarts from Australia by the name of AC/DC were embarking on what would turn out to be one of the most successful and long-lasting careers that the rock world has ever witnessed!

**Bad Company,
Paul Rodgers**

"Bad Company With Angus" demonstrates their similar approach to riffs, being based on big and thick sounding chord voicings, triads, and slash chords that bridged the gap between blues and hard rock. These guys just needed a Gibson, a Marshall, and a ton of attitude to create some of the greatest riffs in history—true 1970s rock gold!

PERFORMANCE NOTES

As ever, make sure you pay attention to the rests, and experiment with where best to position your fretting-hand thumb: on the first A chord it is cool to have it chilling out on top of the neck (helping to mute the sixth/low E string), but in order to execute that D/A you will probably find it best to lower it to a position closer to a classical guitarist—it will help you achieve the stretch needed by your fretting fingers.

Those cool single-note fills require a hammer-on to get a slippery and greasy feel, so pay particular attention to the transcription.

Above all, don't rush this one—imagine you are the Rolling Stones' Keith Richard or AC/DC's Malcolm Young. A humbucker-laden guitar is your best bet and use enough grunt to on the amp to make it rock, but not too much that the individual strings meld together. Don't worry you metalheads—we'll be piling on the distortion soon enough!

TRIADIC TIPS

This riff is based around some cool slash chords using moveable triad shapes—as well as the "open" G power chord that we will now refer to as the "AC/DC G power chord"!

Again, the tonal center is in A, but rather than present you with more power chords that you've already tried, here are some shapes (or "voicings" to be flash!) that gradually move up the neck, giving you some alternative options to get your creative juices flowing.

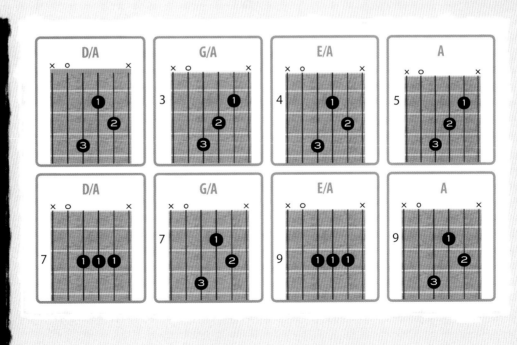

"UP THE IRONS"

In the late 1970s Iron Maiden brought some much-needed aggression and energy into a tired and jaded British rock scene, with a metal style that was inspired by legends such as Black Sabbath and Judas Priest, but played with a punk rock attitude.

Iron Maiden, L–R:
Bruce Dickinson,
Janick Gers, 1993

After their first couple of albums, original singer Paul Di'Anno left to be replaced by the "human air raid siren" that is Bruce Dickinson, and they soon became global superstars.

Rather than look at one particular Maiden track, here we are tackling a riff that combines their trademark "galloping" rhythm with a hint of their classic "Run To The Hills" track from 1982's seminal *Number Of The Beast*.

PERFORMANCE NOTES

"Up The Irons" consists of some root fifth/A string power chords played using lashings of that famed Maiden "galloping" rhythm. Having worked through the previous riffs you won't find fretting the power chords taxing, but pulling off an effective "gallop" is another matter: make sure you listen very carefully to the CD before having a go yourself.

This is a real workout for the picking hand: alternate picking, palm muting—the lot! In particular, make sure the distinction between the normal and the palm muted power chords is clearly audible, as it's the light and shade—the "crunch" and "chug"—that give maximum rock authenticity.

Use your bridge pickup and feel free to pile on the distortion as long as you remember that clarity will win over mush every day of the week.

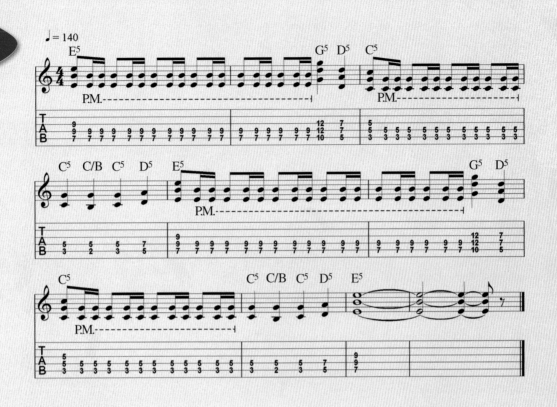

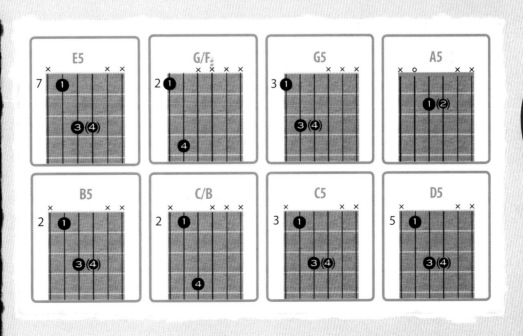

POWER PICKS

"Up The Irons" has been designed as a classic example of a "traditional" hard rock/metal track in E minor, featuring E, F♯, G, A, B, C, and D. These notes form the basis for all the power chords here: earlier metal bands tended to stick within defined keys, whereas more recent acts such as Slipknot, Trivium, and Avenged Sevenfold, adopt a more "anything goes" approach to song writing. So play around and try some classic Maiden-esque riffs of your own!

"DOWN TO PANAMA"

What can you say about Van Halen? "It's Party Time!" This California-based hard rock band injected some much-needed fun into rock and metal when they exploded on the scene in 1978 and changed guitar playing forever.

Van Halen, L–R: David Lee Roth, Eddie Van Halen

This riff takes as its cue the song "Panama" from their amazing multi-million-selling album *1984*, which, along with Van Halen "I," is probably their defining moment. It doesn't matter what generation you are, if you are serious about rock guitar, you owe it to yourself to get these albums. *1984* also features the world-famous smash hit single "Jump" as well as ace tracks such as "Hot For Teacher" and "Top Jimmy" and is a smorgasbord of six-string virtuosity. The fame of Eddie's "two-handed tapping" technique (see Chapter Ten) often overshadows the fact that he's one of the very best rock rhythm guitarists ever to have walked the planet… "Down To Panama" is a pastiche focusing on his great approach to using triads: so grab your spandex and let's hightail it back to the 1980s!

PERFORMANCE NOTES

Once you've internalized the basic triad shapes, make sure both hands are in synch to deal with their rhythmic and muting responsibilities. The picking hand has to adopt a relaxed (you're almost bouncing between picking the triads and skipping over the A/fifth string to chug on those low E notes) yet controlled action, while the fretting hand has to deal with lateral movement up and down the neck. Apply some hefty palm muting on that sixth/low E and really snap out the triads to highlight the tonal difference between the crunch of the triads and the chug of the open string.

Create a fairly heavily overdriven tone with a good amount of bottom end—it will generate that chug on the sixth/low E string, as well as generate richness on the triads. Use less gain than initially you think you need: it's cool at a bedroom practice level—but when you start playing with a drummer "for real," being too reliant on fizzy preamp tone will relegate you to the ranks of being of a YouTube bedroom guitarist.

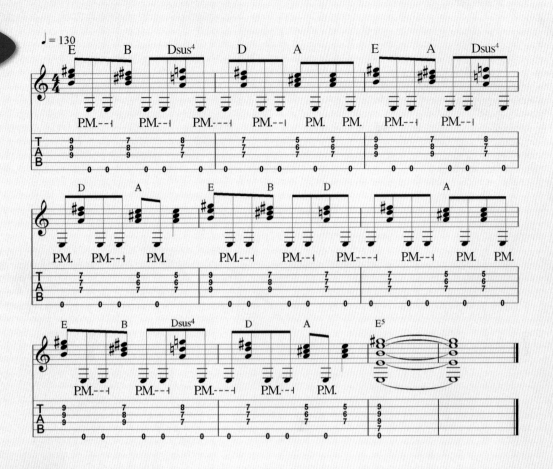

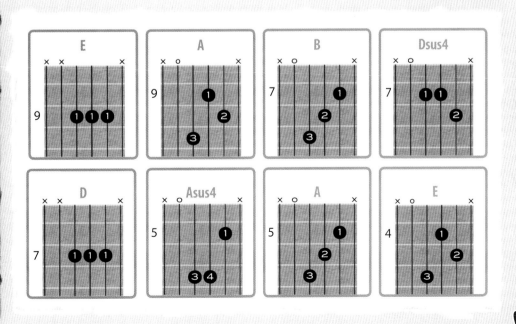

TRIADIC TIPS

"Down To Panama" has a tonal center of E (as you might have guessed by the heavy use of the sixth/low E string within the riff) and utilizes some cool triad shapes that we've expanded upon here for you to get riffing with. These are just a few options to enable you to try a Van Halen-style track of your own.

"RIDE THE METALLICA"

Now established as the biggest heavy metal band of all time, Metallica have been releasing albums since 1983 and this riff looks back to their early years.

Metallica, L–R: Kirk Hammett, James Hetfield

1984's *Ride The Lightning* and 1986's *Master Of Puppets* albums have been the main inspiration for "Ride The Metallica"—a mid-tempo power chord-driven slice of metal. These albums were very obviously influenced by 1970s metal gods Black Sabbath and Judas Priest, and although in the last 20 years Metallica have eclipsed their heroes as far as record sales go, their debt to the original metal masters remains to this day.

PERFORMANCE NOTES

The whole essence of Metallica and fellow thrash metal titans such as Megadeth is a brutal yet massively accurate rhythmic approach that combines aggressive palm muting (see Chapter Two) interspersed with tightly executed power chords and razor-sharp single-note lines.

"Ride the Metallica" uses standard power chords pedaling off a heavily palm muted sixth/low E string. If this sounds too weak by itself (and if you are using a budget amp it probably does), a trick you can utilize to add that thrash metal "chug" to the sixth/low E is to finger a full E5 power chord—but not specifically target the fifth/A string or fourth/D string fretted notes; rather, ensure that your palm is aggressively positioned for muting all three strings, dig in hard on the

picking, and don't worry about being too accurate in just hitting that low E.

This way, while the low E is the dominant musical force here, you are also getting added firepower in the old chug stakes from incidentally hitting the other two strings. It's all about attack and tightly controlled aggression.

This is more effective than simply piling in the gain—unless you have a Diezal or Mesa Boogie Rectifier amp set on "stun" at stadium concert volume levels!

Technically this is fairly straightforward: get comfortable with the individual power chord changes first, then make sure you can hit them with enough attack to ensure they sound like a marauding army, and make sure that the sixth/low E string open notes are pummeled into

muted oblivion… OK, enough war references already!

Tonally, the classic thrash metal sound is a "scooped" one: if you have a basic practice amp, max out your bass and treble controls and zero your mid. That will get you in the right ball park for playing along with the CD.

However, bear in mind that when you're ready to play "for real"—i.e., with a band and a real drummer—those mids are what give you the girth to cut through sonically. Too little and you will be lost over the frequencies generated by the bass guitar and the drums.

It's one of those eternal tonal dilemmas that all metal guitarists face…

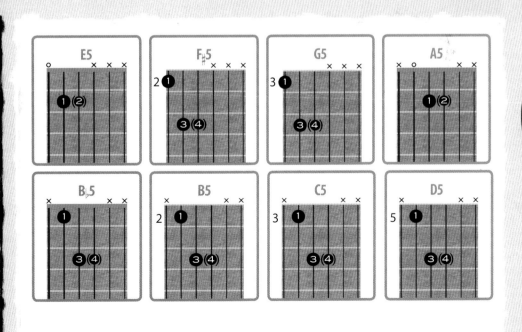

"SMELLS LIKE NIRVANA"

Nirvana exploded onto the international scene in the early 1990s, bursting out of Seattle and spearheading the "grunge" movement that shook the established rock world in a way that no band or music style had done since the punk rock explosion of the mid 1970s.

Nirvana, L–R: Dave Grohl, Kurt Cobain, Krist Novoselic

With socially aware, angst-ridden lyrical themes as well as an anti technique attitude to guitar playing that was the polar opposite to the polished perfection of the 1980s, grunge ruled the rock world for several years in the 1990s.

A whole generation of hair metal and melodic rock bands suddenly found themselves out of work, and while grunge has ultimately not proved as long-lasting as classic rock or metal, the movement's "abandon all rules" approach to music-making deserves consideration. It is also worth noting that many world-famous classic rock and metal outfits were undeniably influenced by the "Seattle sound" (Pearl Jam, Soundgarden, and Alice in Chains also struck commercial gold) and started applying a grungier approach to their riffs—so let's look at an example inspired by that great grunge anthem "Smells Like Teen Spirit."

PERFORMANCE NOTES

The changes are very simple; what is important is the energy and momentum of the riff—and what keeps this driving is the rhythmic movement in between the power chords. To execute this, simply keep the picking hand strumming even when you are switching between the individual power chords. However, don't let the fretting hand lose all contact with the strings or you will get a mess. Keep physical contact with the strings loose—not actually fretting the strings but applying fretting-hand muting. This will get a "clicky" sound similar to that used by funk guitarists, but with distortion and an almost reckless, "attacking" approach, you'll add rhythmic energy to the riff.

Unlike many riffs in this book, we are not after cleanliness of technique—this is all about attitude, the essence of rock.

Again, tonally, go for a decent amount of overdrive with this riff, but do not apply too much gain.

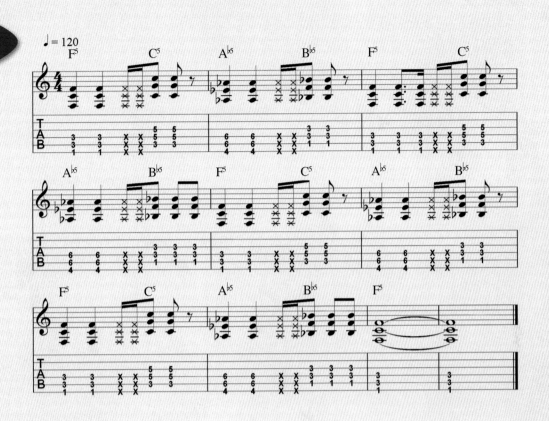

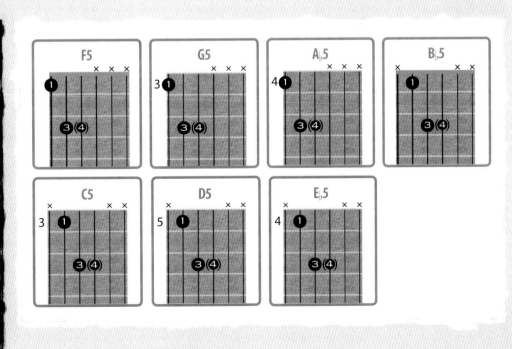

"BLINK ON A GREEN DAY"

In the late 1990s a whole load of bands took the basic essence of the mid-1970s punk rock ethos, and injected more of a party rock atmosphere designed to put the fun back into rock.

Green Day, Billie Joe Armstrong, 2005

As grunge supplanted the melodic and hair metal scene several year previously, so the "Rock Wheel of Fortune" spun again, and bands such as Green Day, Sum 41, Blink-182, New Found Glory, and Good Charlotte likewise blew away the mental navel gazing that the Seattle scene liked to indulge in. Suddenly it was cool to have fun again—and these bands sold millions!

PERFORMANCE NOTES

This one's all about sheer tempo (the basic changes should be simple enough, being basic power chords) so it's only a question of having enough speed and "muscle memory" to execute the changes.

When trying to master speedy riffs such as this one, it is vital to keep your fretting hand relaxed (so you can "bounce" off the strings) as well as keeping your picking hand smooth enough that you keep the rhythm consistent.

The same basic rules that you've already encountered with "Smells Like Nirvana" regarding the "bits between the chords" apply: but with such a quick tempo the percussive "clicks" are simply played in quarter notes, backing up the kick drum and keeping the riff driving in the absence of the chords. Go for some decent overdrive here, and a trebly tone to cut through at these higher tempos.

A lot of bands in this genre operate almost exclusively in major keys, as the upbeat and brighter sound is more suited to their generally lighthearted musical approach, rather than the more somber minor keys that almost all metal bands prefer. "Blink On A Green Day" has power chords exclusively from the key of C major (C, D, E, F, G, A, B), so here's the full key of C arranged for power chords. Oh, and don't forget to have fun!

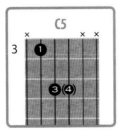

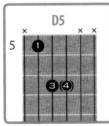

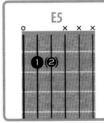

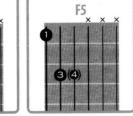

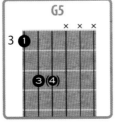

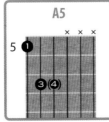

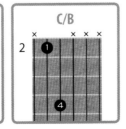

Alternative band plays club set

CHAPTER SIX:
LET'S ROCK

Over the course of the last two chapters we've looked at riffs that are based primarily on chords and triads, but no doubt you've noticed that several of them have also featured single notes amidst all that chordal mayhem. In this chapter we're going to concentrate on riffs where scales and single note lines take precedence.

For this chapter we've produced six riffs inspired by classic songs from the 1960s to the 1990s, that will get you used to playing single-note-based riffs down near the nut—i.e., the lower end of the fretboard, keeping things low 'n' mean.

Playing scales lower down the neck requires a different mental and physical approach to playing solos or licks up in "soloing territory"—i.e., higher up the neck. The string tension is subtly different, and for many players it can be a pain dealing with those pesky open strings, but it's worth it for the richness of tone and ease of notes that those open strings can offer.

PERFORMANCE NOTES

These sections provide advice for any areas likely to give specific difficulty, as well as a guide to what sound settings you should have on your amp and guitar.

SCALEWISE

These sections are designed to get you straight into the creative process and get you coming up with your own riffs and songs by focusing on what scales have been used as well as covering tonal centers, keys, and some songwriting tips where appropriate.

Having an awareness of the "theory" involved gives you some immediate options should you wish to come up with some riffs of your own in a similar style—but it's very doubtful that any of the artists featured here ever thought "Hey, today I'm gonna write a kick-ass riff in A minor"!

Almost invariably what they would have done is simply noodled around on the guitar and suddenly stumbled upon something that caught their attention. Through their years of playing they would have gained an innate knowledge of what notes work well together—but our mission here is to get you trained up *now*, thus saving years of fumbling around the fretboard. Knowing your scales simply gives you more freedom and less constraint, so embrace them folks—they really do help!

SCALETASTIC RIFF WARRIORS

Almost every rock band in history has used scales as a basis for their riffs and songs at some point. Used on its own, a scale-based riff can seem less powerful than simply piling in with the power chords, but ever since pivotal moments such as The Beatles' "Ticket To Ride" they have become part of the rock guitarist's musical arsenal. Led Zeppelin's Jimmy Page was particularly partial to these—"Rock'n' Roll" and "Black Dog" spring immediately to mind—helped massively by the legendary rhythm section of John Bonham and John Paul Jones who provided the musical back-up power to his riffs.

Right: The Beatles on British TV's *Top of the Pops* in 1966. This phase of their career was a pivotal time in rock history

"ERIC'S SUNSHINE"

Cream were the legendary three-piece that Eric Clapton formed with Jack Bruce and Ginger Baker in the mid to late 1960s and their improvisational approach to live gigs, bludgeoning riffs, and long, virtuosic solos helped lay the foundations for the heavy rock and metal supergroups of the 1970s.

Cream, Eric Clapton, 1968

"Eric's Sunshine" takes its inspiration from arguably Cream's most famous track "Sunshine of Your Love," which was one of the first songs to take the humble blues scale and twist it into something more sinister.

The original is based upon notes from the D minor blues scale (see "Scalewise") played mainly using the position 1 shape at the tenth fret:

However "Eric's Sunshine" uses an extended shape combining positions 2 and 3 which is played down the bottom of the neck:

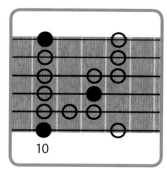

10

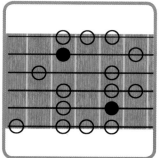

This involves more lateral—i.e., moving along the strings—and shifts than the original, so take your time and get comfortable with the basic shapes.

There are also a couple of power chords built from the fourth/D string.

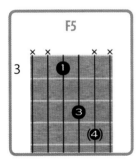

F5

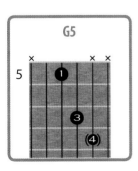

G5

PERFORMANCE NOTES

Listen carefully to the CD before tackling this one, paying close attention to the rests—most fall on the "off beat"—i.e. the gaps between the beat, creating tension.

Sit in tight with the bass guitar on this one. To gain depth and power, many scale based riffs have the bass doubling exactly what the guitar is playing.

Slide between the power chords: play the G5 as normal and then, keeping the shape and finger pressure intact, slide down to the third fret. Take your time: if your grip is too tight your fingers will feel almost glued to the fifth fret and sliding with prove difficult… too relaxed and you'll lose the notes.

Dial in overdrive here to sustain the notes, but not too much or it will lose definition. If using single coil pickups, use the neck pickup to add depth, although on the CD I used the bridge pickup.

SCALEWISE

This riff is in the key of D minor, and the scale of choice here is the D minor blues scale (D, F, G, A♭, A, C.) If you want to expand upon this when experimenting, feel free to combine it with the D minor scale, which will give you a couple of extra notes—E and B♭—to add in.

As an exercise I'll leave it to you to work out where these are.

"FUNK YOUR EMOTION"

In the early 1970s Aerosmith blasted out of Boston and brought with them a real sense of groove and funk to the rock genre. Now established members of the rock superstar aristocracy, guitarists Joe Perry and Brad Whitford's playing has always leant more towards groove and rhythmic interplay rather than the solo flights of fancy of many of their peers.

Taking their cues from the Rolling Stones, they created music that had an elasticity of rhythm which clearly separated them from the more straight-ahead rhythmic approach of their peers. "Walk This Way" (a hit in the 1970s, and again in the 1980s with their collaboration with rappers Run-DMC) and "Sweet Emotion" are near-perfect examples of groove-based rock that just made you want to hit the dancefloor. This combination of funk and rock influenced a whole host of bands—check out Wild Cherry's "Play That Funky Music" as well as the rockier songs from Minnesota superstar Prince.

"Funk Your Emotion" uses notes solely from the E minor pentatonic scale, played down near the nut using positions 1 and 2:

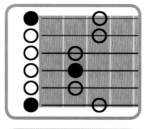

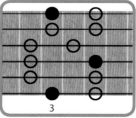

3

Aerosmith, L–R:
Steven Tyler, Joe Perry

SCALEWISE

This riff is based purely on the notes from the E minor pentatonic scale (E, G, A, B, D). If you want to expand upon this and add in some more notes or power chords of your own, then you're probably best trying the E dorian mode:

E F♯ G A B C♯ D

If you feel like adding some chords, refer to "Whole Lotta Led" and experiment with those—they should fit in with the groove we've got going here.

PERFORMANCE NOTES

As with all the riffs in this chapter, listen carefully to the CD before tackling this. The basic notes are easy enough to execute, but getting that groove will take quite some time. There's a real sense of "swing" to this riff, and the phrasing approach is much more "funk" than you are probably used to. This requires a quite different mental and physical approach to your standard rock riffs: it's much less "on the beat." Your picking hand needs to be more relaxed and your whole

approach looser than, for example, pounding out an Iron Maiden or Black Sabbath riff. Metal-based players are often very "straight" rhythmically, which is great for nailing your typical metal riffs—but when called upon to relax and "groove," they lose it!

It's as much a mental thing as a physical one. You need to relax your whole approach, worrying less about the notes and more about the rhythm. It's an established fact that the average listener

will put up with wrong notes played in the right rhythm far more than they will accept the right notes played rhythmically incorrectly.

Even if you aspire to be the heaviest death metal overlord and never want to "funk it up," never underestimate the ability to groove and play rhythmically. Rhythm is the glue that holds the whole thing together: ignore this at your peril!

Tonally, go for a snarly overdrive playing and use the bridge pickup.

"OZZY'S TRAIN"

When Ozzy Osbourne left Black Sabbath in 1979, few could have foreseen the success that he would achieve as a solo artist. *Blizzard Of Ozz*, his comeback album released in 1980, brought to the world's attention the amazing Randy Rhoads.

Randy Rhoads, 1980

Randy Rhoads was a diminutive blond Californian guitar god who shook up a guitar scene still reeling from Eddie Van Halen's meteoric rise. Taking his cues as much from composers such as Bach as his rock guitar predecessors, Randy introduced a classical element to metal guitar, expanding on the hybrid of rock and classical music hybrid that Ritchie Blackmore and Uli Jon Roth had explored in the 1970s.

Tragically killed in a plane crash in 1982, Randy left us a legacy of guitar playing that still resonates today.

"Ozzy's Train" takes its cue from "Crazy Train" and utilizes the same $F_\sharp$ minor scale played in position one as the basis for the riff.

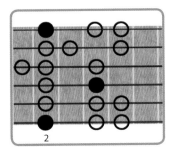

2

PERFORMANCE NOTES

Here's one for you metallers: no wimpy off-beat notes with this one! Simple eighth notes in a repeated scale sequence provides the basis for this riff. As the tempo isn't too speedy, you can either play this "correctly" with alternate picking, or—if you want to add some beef and metal attack—down-pick the hell out of it!

SCALEWISE

Like "Crazy Train," this riff is based purely on the notes from the F♯ minor scale (F♯, G♯, A, B, C♯, D) so this is your starting point when expanding the ideas here and coming up with your own Ozzy-esque riffs.

If you wish to include some power chords then the safest ones to use are those simply built from each of the scale's notes—you should be able to locate them yourself by now! To stay strictly "in key" use an A/G♯ "altered" power chord instead of a standard G♯ power chord—but both work equally well in most situations.

"BEAT IT JACKSON"

Michael Jackson released the biggest selling album in history in 1983: *Thriller* was an unprecedented—and probably never to be repeated—success. Fusing elements of funk, balladry, disco, and rock, the album crossed all barriers—and a million guitarists freaked out when they heard "Beat It!"

Steve Lukather

The guitar solo by Eddie Van Halen is a veritable master class—but arguably the most famous element is the main riff.

Renowned Los Angeles session guitarist extraordinaire Steve Lukather (pictured left) played the famous main riff, and "Beat It Jackson" is built along very similar lines, being based around the E minor scale in the open position.

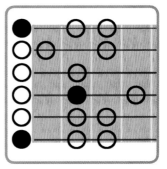

PERFORMANCE NOTES

Pretty straightforward this one: to execute this with sufficient accuracy just concentrate on locking in with the drums and bass guitar. Probably the hardest thing to incorporate are the quick "power slides" but as they're for added expression, you might want to concentrate on nailing the basic riff first, and then insert the slides when you are confident enough.

SCALEWISE

This track is in E minor, so to expand upon the riff experiment using any notes from the E minor scale (E, F#, G, A, B, C, D) and flip back to "Up the Irons" to find the power chords available in this key. Remember, all of these are only suggestions (if you use these as a basis, almost anything you play will sound "right") but you can always throw caution to the wind, chuck out all this "theory," and try something completely random… You might just come up with something great that "theoretically" shouldn't work. It may be a cliché, but it's true: it's not what you play, it's how you play it.

"ENTER METALLICA"

Another riff inspired by metal leviathans Metallica, this takes its cue from the lead track—"Enter Sandman"—of the mega-selling *Black* album released in 1991.

Metallica,
James Hetfield

With its Spinal Tap-esque "none more black" cover, this album propelled Metallica into the stratosphere, selling millions and firmly establishing Metallica as the most successful metal band in history.

"Enter Metallica" is based around the E minor blues scale, played mainly in position 3, with a healthy sprinkling of open E string notes to add depth.

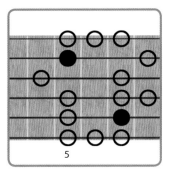

5

PERFORMANCE NOTES

Another one for you metallers: this combines a true metal approach with more groove than many famed metal riffs. Again, nothing too demanding technically with this one—it's more about locking in very tightly to the drums and bass with almost surgical precision. Make sure you palm mute as heavily as possible with down-picks on the power chords to gain an authentic metallic chug.

SCALEWISE

"Enter Metallica" is based on the notes from the E minor blues scale (E G A B♭, B D) and its sense of menace results from honing in on the ♭5 note—B♭. The ♭5 interval is known as the *diabolus in musica*—"the devil in music"—a term coined by the Church hundreds of years ago. It is an important interval and one that has an almost schizophrenic personality: played adjacent to its neighbors the fourth and fifth, it just sounds cool and bluesy; played in isolation as a main melody note, it imparts a sense of disorientation and doom.

If you want to expand upon this to create some variations of your own, you could do worse than adding in the notes from the standard E minor scale as well:

E, F♯, G, A, B, C, D

This will give you a full eight notes to play with creating a (flashy technical term here folks!) "hybrid scale."

E, F♯, G, A, B♭, B, C, D

The full range of power chords at your disposal from these are shown in the earlier Metallica track "Ride The Metallica," so flip back a few pages to refresh your memory.

To really boost the "evil" atmosphere you could try using an F5 as well: using "wrong" power chords is standard practice in the heavier styles of music as it's not so rigidly based upon "normal" key structures.

What all this means is that—despite all this talk about tonal centers, keys, scales, and the rest—sometimes you can use anything, as long as it sounds cool…

CHAPTER SEVEN:
PHRASING TECHNIQUES AND HOT LICKS

In this chapter we will be applying a ton of cool techniques to the minor pentatonic scale, which will really shift your playing up a gear. We will also look at some essential guitar licks; master these and eventually you'll be soloing like a seasoned pro.

LICK EXERCISES

Let's face it, it's the sound of a burning electric guitar solo that got most of us hooked, and the first step to developing your ability to play hot solos is building up a decent vocabulary of cool licks.

Most licks will combine a variety of different playing techniques within a single phrase—be it bending, vibrato, hammer-ons, pull-offs, or whatever.

The best way to prepare yourself for getting some cool licks integrated into your playing is to isolate the core techniques needed and master them one at a time, rather than jumping in at the deep end and attempting some hot lick straight off. You'll only get frustrated—so take the time now and reap the rewards later on.

The most commonly used scale for playing cool licks and solos in the early years of most guitarists' playing is the standard minor pentatonic. In fact, there are a ton of guitarists out there who have developed successful professional or semi-professional careers having never ventured much further than this humble scale—so never underestimate the power of the pentatonic!

While this can be played in many different ways, by far the most common licks are to be found in the position 1 shape.

All the exercises in this chapter are in A minor, a much favored rock key:

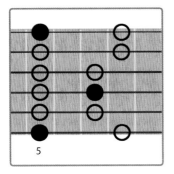

PENTATONIC PERFECTION

Masters of the pentatonic scale abound, but make sure you've checked out Eric Clapton, Jimi Hendrix, David Gilmour, Jimmy Page, Brian May, Michael Shenker, Stevie Ray Vaughan, Eric Johnson, Zakk Wylde, and Joe Bonamassa.

HAMMER-ONS AND PULL-OFFS

Hammer-ons and pull-offs provide a great tonal alternative to picking every note: they produce a smoother and less "mechanical" sound—and are absolutely integral to rock music.

You have already tackled these, both specifically as exercises in Chapter Three and sporadically throughout the riff examples covered to date. The following exercises take a two-string "cell" from the minor pentatonic, specifically the fifth to seventh frets of the fourth/D and third/G strings.

Exercise 1 utilizes hammer-ons. Be careful not to rush the hammered note—all the notes should be of the same duration. People new to this are often in such a hurry to try out this new technique that they forget about the timing.

TRACK
60

Exercise 2 utilizes pull-offs. Don't be in a rush to pull off that note or the end result will be messy and uneven. It may be an idea to pick all the notes from these exercises first, to imprint the timing in your brain before adding in the hammer-ons and pull-offs.

TRACK
61

TECHNICAL NOTE

You will probably find the hammer-ons easier to execute. Common problems with pull-offs include the downward motion of your third finger dragging the index finger slightly toward the floor, causing that second note to become slightly sharp. This creates an undesirable cat-like "meow." There is no quick way around this other than vigilance: make sure that your first finger is anchored securely enough to resist moving. The flipside of this coin is that if you apply too much pressure, your hand and fingers will lock up… but then, no one ever said it would be easy! Be aware of these potential pitfalls and adjust your playing accordingly.

Exercise 3 combines both techniques to create a continuous flowing phrase. Only approach when Exercises 1 and 2 are well integrated…

Exercise 4 is similar to Exercise 3, but played in triplets: count "1&a, 2&a, 3&a, 4&a" consistently to ensure no rushing and timing errors. Taking this very structured and methodical approach now will reap real dividends later on, I promise!

Exercise 5 simply takes the full A minor pentatonic position 1 and plays it using hammer-ons when ascending and pull-offs when descending, in a constant eighth-note pattern. There will be a real natural inclination to rush this, so work hard to keep this in check. As ever, count!

Exercise 6 introduces a "scale sequence." Sequencing is when you take a basic pattern of notes and replicate that throughout the strings/scale shape. Scale sequences are very important in soloing and improvising and, used correctly, they can really help form a structure to your improvising and stop it sounding like vacuous noodling around.

TRACK
65

Exercise 7 reverses the same pattern.

TRACK
66

Exercise 8 takes the full A minor pentatonic position 1 and plays it using hammer-ons when ascending, and pull-offs when descending—but this time to a triplet count.

TRACK
67

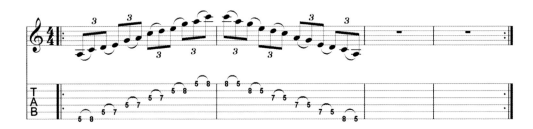

Exercise 9 introduces a real classic, much loved by players such as Jimmy Page, in which we descend the A minor pentatonic position 1 in groups of three notes, to a triplet rhythm.

TRACK
68

Finally, Exercise 10 reverses the same pattern…

TRACK
69

HAMMER-ON HEROES AND PULL-OFF PROS

Jimmy Page needs particular attention as a master of minor pentatonic hammer-ons and pull-offs, as does Michael Shenker and indeed super-shredder Paul Gilbert (pictured right).

SLIPPIN' AN' SLIDIN' AWAY

Slides are a great and relatively easy technique to master. Sonically, they are in the same ballpark as hammer-ons and pull-offs, smoothing the transition between notes.

Slides are particularly effective when executing licks that span several frets on one string, or shifting between scale positions, as they reduce the need for large fretting-hand stretches.

These exercises look at sliding between adjacent notes from the minor pentatonic. Try them first with the index finger; then, to make sure that you are fully prepared for future cool licks, practice the same exercises with your second and third fingers.

It goes without saying that you must adhere to all those picking- and fretting-hand principles which, by now, should be fully engrained.

The final slide takes a wilder approach, sliding quickly from the fourteenth to the seventh fret on the G string. These long-distance slides can be tricky to master, as it is hard to stop in time: you can easily overshoot the destination fret. In truth, these slides are beyond the remit of this book—but what the hell: give it a go!

The best way of approaching these slides is to get your finger in position for the first note, then keep your eyes fixed on the target second note. Don't try to follow the slide down as you will get in all sorts of mess! Just go for it.

This sort of slide is often used more as an effect than as part of a melody (although they feature prominently in the work of players such as Steve Vai) but they are great at adding excitement.

POWER SLIDES

These simply rule when you need to make a grand entrance, either for the beginning of a song or the opening of a solo. Check out John Sykes's intro to Whitesnake's "Still Of The Night" for an example of one of the ultimate power slides. A power slide is basically a bass string (usually the sixth /low E) slide from around the fifteenth fret area, picked good and hard, and then slid down the neck, gradually releasing pressure (and hence the note) until you are hovering around the lower regions of the fretboard. These are pretty hard to notate—so listen hard to the CD.

These two examples are standard power slides leading to E5 and A5 power chords: simple, but devastatingly effective! Few things are more "rock" than these babies!

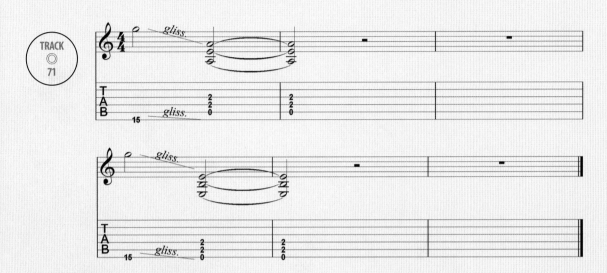

SLIDING SOPHISTICATION

All these individual techniques are integral to almost every guitarist's playing, but you particularly need to check out the aforementioned Steve Vai as well as the ubiquitous Eddie Van Halen, George Lynch, Steve Lukather (pictured right), and Greg Howe. Tony Iommi, John Sykes, and Zakk Wylde are masters of creating monstrously powerful power slides.

PHRASING TECHNIQUES

BENDING

The ability to bend strings and smoothly raise one note to another is one of the great characteristics of the guitar. Bending helps to provide a vocal quality to your playing and, particularly when combined with vibrato (see opposite), adds real personality. Bending came to the fore when electric guitarists such as Eric Clapton started using thinner-gauge strings and replacing the previously wound G with unwound strings. These thinner strings, with their reduced tension, made bending the strings easier, and in no time at all a whole new rock vocabulary was established.

It is possible to raise the pitch of a note by either pushing the string upward toward the ceiling, or downward toward the floor. We will look at bending solely on the treble strings, which are best played by pushing the string upward, particularly on the first and second strings: pull the string toward the floor on these two and you will quickly find that you dragged the string off the fretboard—a quirky, but not massively desirable, effect.

There are a few things to watch out for:
• Excess string noise is mostly dealt with using the fretting- and picking-hand muting and control skills you have begun to master, but there is the added complication that you are pushing a string out of its normal "zone," into the areas normally occupied by the strings directly physically above. This can mean that those strings will slip out of your control, generating all manner of extraneous noise. This is perfectly normal, and it will take time and effort to get used to being extra-vigilant in the controlling of the strings.
• You might also find that those strings slip up and over the tips of your fingers, sliding happily away over your nails. Don't worry if this happens: in time you will gain the ability the push those strings upward without getting under them.
• To help train your ears, play the initial note, pause, then play the "target" note before trying the following bends. That way you will have provided an aural reference point so you know when to stop bending.
• Don't rush: often people are so eager to bend that they start the movement almost before they've struck the initial note. Doing this means that the whole thing will sound a bit "seasick." You need to have that first note clear so that when you reach the target note it feels resolved and a complete musical phrase.

The following exercise looks at four very common bends from the A minor pentatonic.

Bending from the seventh to the ninth fret of the third/G string, which raises a D to an E. The tension on this string is pretty loose, so you shouldn't find this one too hard. Fret the seventh fret with your third finger, and have the first and second fingers behind it to add strength and support.

TRACK
72.1

Bending from the eighth to the tenth fret of the second/B string, which raises a G to an A. The tension on this string is a bit tougher, so you will need to apply more effort. Fret the eighth fret with your third finger, and again have the first and second fingers behind it to add strength and support.

TRACK
◎
72.2

Bending from the fifteenth to the seventeenth fret of the same second/B string, which raises a D to an E. The higher you are on this string, the easier it is to bend, so adjust your effort accordingly. Try not to "overshoot" or it will sound out of tune. Again, use all three fingers. Using more than one finger is known as assisted bending and provides much more strength and accuracy than flailing around trying to perform these with only one finger. You should not attempt any of these exercises using just one finger. However, there will be times when you need to bend with only two fingers, so try the next two exercises with your first and second finger as well to prepare yourself.

TRACK
◎
72.3

Finally, bending from the fifteenth to the seventeenth fret of the first/E string, which raises a G to an A. Despite this being the thinnest string, the tension is stiffer than the other two we've looked at—so really dig in with this one!

TRACK
◎
72.4

VIBRATO

Vibrato on the guitar is generally defined as the raising and releasing of a pitch by either pushing a string upward or pulling it downward in a rhythmic fashion. Vibrato is perhaps the greatest way to add expression and emotion to your playing. It is one of the true definers of a good guitarist—and also one of hardest things to master. There are legions of super-fast guitarists out there who can perform death-defying feats on the fretboard, yet have a weak and undefined vibrato.

Vibrato is also amazingly individualistic. You can identify many of the greatest rock guitarists in history within a couple of notes by their vibrato: from BB King, Eric Clapton, Brian May, Jeff Beck, and David Gilmour through to Steve Vai and Yngwie Malmsteen: all are defined by their amazing and unique vibrato. The intensity, speed, and pitch range varies from player to player, so experiment, and really listen to your own favorite players.

It takes most guitarists years to develop an authentic vibrato, but by including this in your practice schedule now, you will be one step ahead—so let's get you milking those notes like a pro!

This exercise looks again at several notes which you will find yourself adding vibrato on whenever you are playing in the key of A minor.

TRACK
73

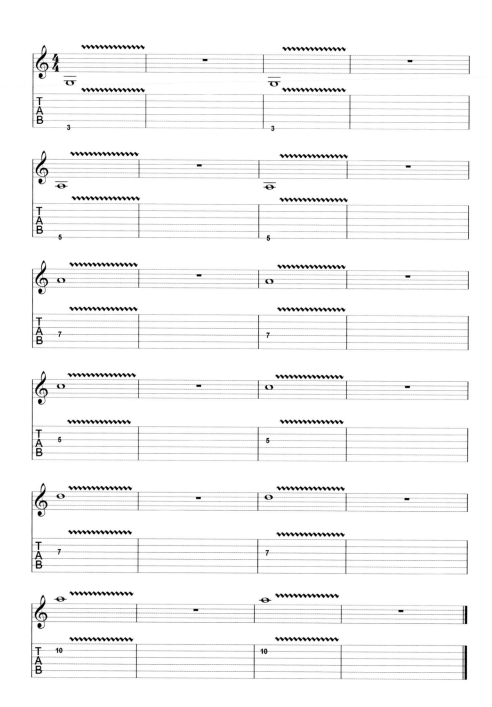

VIBRANT VIBRATO

When applying vibrato to any note, your choice of which finger or fingers to use will depend upon where you have come from, or indeed where you are going: so for all of these, try just your first finger, then fret the notes with your second finger—but add back up with your first—before finally fretting the note with your third finger and then having both the first and second fingers assisting this.

Initially you will find it easier to apply vibrato by pulling the string—indeed, that is your only option on the sixth/low E string—but bear in mind that vibrato can equally be performed by pushing the string (which, conversely, is your only option on the first/top E string!) … so (and you've guessed it again!) do both.

A word of warning: do not actively push/pull the string back to normal: let the natural tension of the string take you back. If you actively push/pull the string back, you will probably overshoot the "neutral zone," and this will end up making your vibrato sound decidedly ill!

BENDING AND VIBRATO

Here's the biggie: the technique that will make you sound like a true rock guitar hero. Applying vibrato to a note that you've already bent up, then maintaining the new note's pitch, is something that can defeat the aspiring guitarist. The following takes the same bending exercises we looked at a couple of pages back and simply applies vibrato. I say simply, but this technique is arguably the hardest physically to master in the entire book so don't expect an instant result!

First get comfortable with bending the string to the target note, then apply vibrato by pushing the string a stage farther, then release it back to the target note, push it a stage farther, release to the target note, and repeat the process again and again. Your ears are crucial to this—but also be aware that they can let you down. You will be so caught up in bending the string and controlling all those other strings that sometimes your ears will take a backseat. The easiest way to deal with this is to record your efforts, take a break, then come back and listen to what you produced. Be very strict with yourself: Is it too "quavery"? Is it uneven in how far you push the string (known as the width of vibrato)? Is it varying widely in speed?

BLINDING BENDING, VIRTUOSO VIBRATO

The usual suspects apply: Eric Clapton, Jeff Beck, David Gilmour, and Brian May are supreme masters—as are Eddie Van Halen, Gary Moore, Steve Lukather, Warren DeMartini, George Lynch, Yngwie Malmsteen, Stevie Ray Vaughan, Joe Satriani, Andy Timmons, and Jeff Kollman.

10 COOL REPEATING LICKS

Here are 10 "repeating licks" that you can use time and again in all manner of musical situations. Whether you're rocking it up or getting all emotional in a ballad, these are endlessly adaptable staples of rock guitar-playing.

Repeating licks are when a basic phrase is repeated several times. Done at the right time and place, they help build continuity into a solo or melody, and can really add intensity and energy to your playing. Repeating licks abound in rock guitar, but if you want a fantastic example, look no farther than Jimmy Page's final phrase at the climax of Led Zeppelin's "Stairway To Heaven" solo, just before the vocals kick in with the immortal line "And as we wind on down the road…" It doesn't get any better than that!

Let's look at that same basic lick idea, albeit an octave lower (that's 12 frets to us guitarists) and played at a slightly more realistic tempo!

TRACK
75.1

Bar your index finger over the fifth fret of the second and first strings, and start with an upstroke on the B string. Play the eighth fret of the first string with a downstroke and pull that note off to the already "pre-fretted" fifth fret of the first string.

Don't worry too much about "note bleed" (that is, the fifth fret notes ringing into each other): at a lower tempo such as this, it gives a cool bit of dirt to the lick; when you have developed sufficient technique to play this at a higher speed, you will find that the very act of playing this fast gets rid of that.

Lick number two takes a basic sixteenth-note rhythm to create a suitably flashy-sounding lick which, once you've got your basic pull-off technique sorted (i.e., you're not continually slipping off the edge of the fretboard), shouldn't be too hard to deal with.

TRACK
◎
75.2

If this feels too scary, get out that dreaded metronome and input a slower speed, something like 60 bpm, and gradually work your way up to the recorded examples. These are all at 100 bpm because that's a good average tempo to set as your goal.

Lick number three is the same as number two, but instead of utilizing the first and second strings, we have now transferred the same basic pattern to the second and third strings: notice that the shape changes as we have to deal with the same scale shape.

TRACK
◎
75.3

Lick number four is a variation of the sort of lick that Chuck Berry made famous in "Johnny B. Goode," albeit on only two strings.

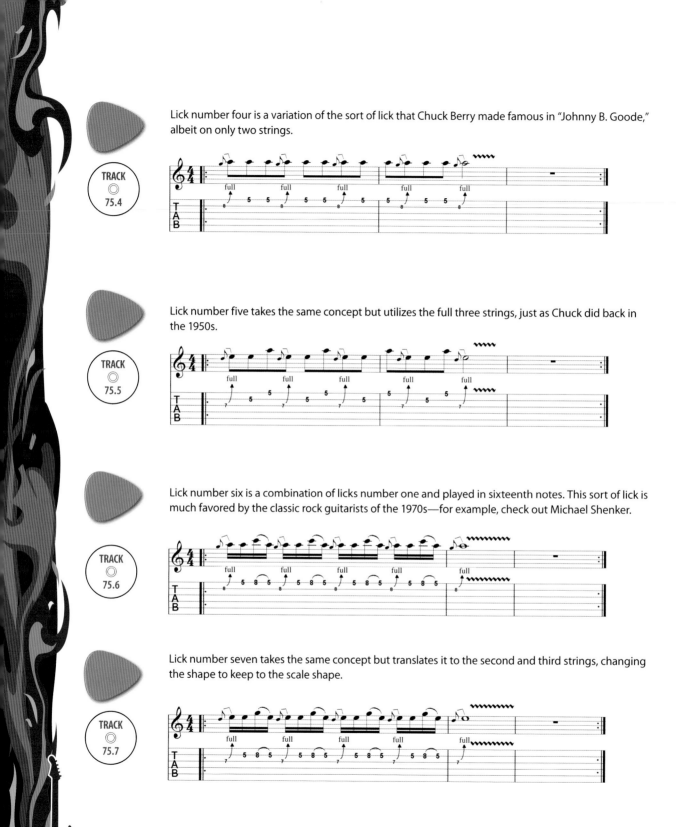

Lick number five takes the same concept but utilizes the full three strings, just as Chuck did back in the 1950s.

Lick number six is a combination of licks number one and played in sixteenth notes. This sort of lick is much favored by the classic rock guitarists of the 1970s—for example, check out Michael Shenker.

Lick number seven takes the same concept but translates it to the second and third strings, changing the shape to keep to the scale shape.

Lick number eight incorporates lick seven and combines it with a four-note descending pattern. The hardest lick here, this is the sort of lick that Slash has made his own, as well as (again) having a distinct Michael Shenker flavor.

TRACK
75.8

Lick number nine is equally effective as a riff or a lick, and Ace Frehley from Kiss utilized this sort of thing regularly in Kiss's 1970s heyday.

TRACK
75.9

Finally, lick number 10 takes the same sort of idea, but, by having consecutive notes played on the third/G string and the fifth/A strings, introduces string skipping. As the name implies, "string skipping" simply involves skipping over an adjacent string from one note to the next). Again equally effective as a lick or a riff, this sort of lick adds a cool rhythmic quality to your improvisations.

TRACK
75.10

"WHEN BILLY MET GEORGE"

TRACK
76

Here is a cool ZZ Top-style rock shuffle in A for you to try to apply all the exercises and licks covered in this chapter. There are no rules here—try what you like in any order, fast, slow, or anything in between: anything goes. Sure, it's going to sound rough at first, but the sooner you can get used to practicing over "real" music, the sooner you can make all these exercises, scales, and licks come together and you'll sound like you're a "real" player—not someone just noodling around with a few exercises. So grab your ax, dial in a cookin' lead tone on your amp, and let rip!

Muse, Matthew Bellamy

CHAPTER EIGHT:
SCALES

Scales... the very word can inspire fear in the budding guitarist, but in reality you have little to be scared of—and they don't have to be boring to learn. Already we have encountered a few scale notes in the riffs, so let's sit back for a chapter and get you used to playing these essential musical tools. Remember all those hot solos that attracted you to the guitar in the first place? Yep, most of them are made up of scales. Luckily, rock music is pretty simple from a scale perspective and you can become a fabulous player by knowing only a few scales.

THE MINOR PENTATONIC

Without a doubt the most commonly used scale in rock, for both riffs and solos, this is simply five notes. *Pente* is Greek for the number five, hence the name.

Remember when we learned the moveable shapes for chords and power chords? We took the same basic shapes and simply moved them up and down the neck depending upon which key was needed. The same thing applies here and all the examples in this chapter are in A.

Position One

TRACK
77.1

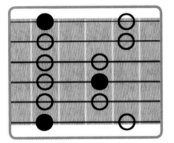

You could play this twelve frets higher as well, so get comfortable with this too:

Position Four

TRACK
77.2

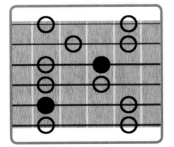

This one is impossible shifted up twelve frets, but played twelve frets lower is cool for some bluesy open-string licks as well as a basis for riffs.

THE MINOR BLUES SCALE

This is basically a minor pentatonic with one extra note, but that note adds a real "bluesy" flavor—hence the name. Be aware, though, that this extra note needs to be treated with caution: it sounds absolutely fab at the right time, but just plain wrong in other situations until you learn how to apply it.

Position One

Again, you can play this twelve frets higher as well...

Position Four

And this one is cool for playing twelve frets lower.

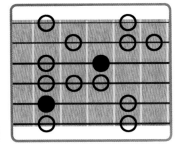

THE MAJOR SCALE

It's important to know how to play this not just for its own sake, but also to learn how other scales and chords are constructed.

In its full form it isn't as commonly used for solos as the minor pentatonic—although it's popular in glam and punk rock as a basis for song construction, and is a big favorite for a certain type of rock anthem. It is also much used in hot rock soundtracks to Hollywood movies—as you will hear on the scale melody example track "Top Steve" (pages 140–1). This is the first example we've looked at that is a "true" scale—in that it has seven notes (theory stuff you can ignore for the time being!).

Position One

TRACK
79.1

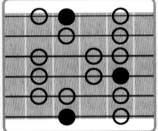

Position Four

TRACK
79.2

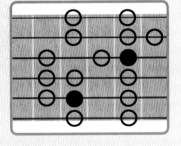

THE MINOR SCALE

The minor scale is much used as a basis for metal because of its suitably dark tonality, but is also a popular choice for ballads, so this is an important scale to get comfortable with. Like the major scale, it has the full seven notes. As with the minor pentatonic and minor blues scales, experiment shifting these twelve frets higher and lower.

Position One

TRACK
80.1

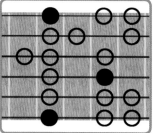

Position Four

TRACK
80.2

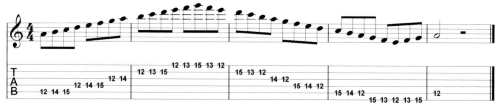

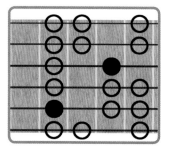

THREE-NOTES-PER-STRING PATTERNS

These shapes are great for solo lines, and make perfect picking exercises because they have the same number of notes on each string—so once you get a pattern established, you simply replicate it through the entire scale shape.

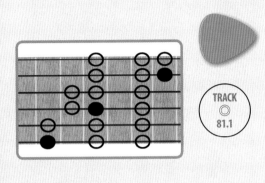

Major scale root sixth/low E string shape

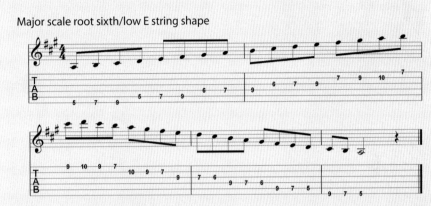

TRACK
81.1

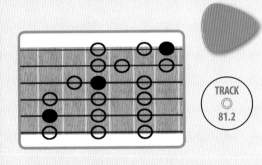

Major scale root fifth/A string shape

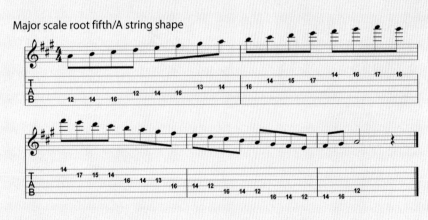

TRACK
81.2

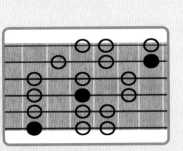

Minor scale root sixth/low E string shape

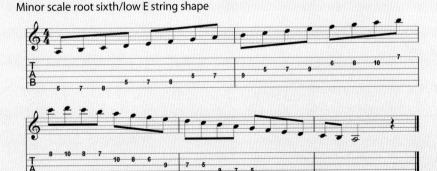

TRACK
82.1

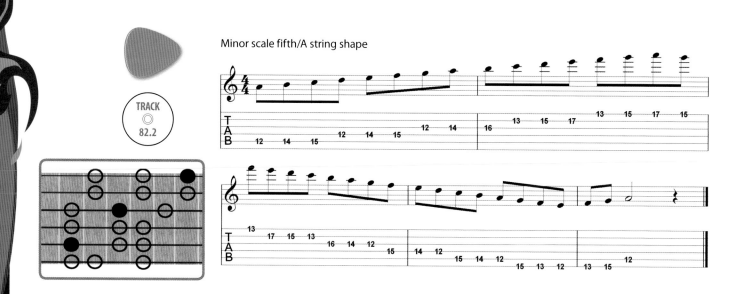

Minor scale fifth/A string shape

TRACK
82.2

MAKING MUSIC
MELODIES AND MELODIC SOLOING

The purpose of these examples is to reinforce the fact that despite all this talk about licks and techniques, our primary function as guitarists is to be musicians and to play "music"—and melodies (or tunes) are the purest example of music.

Now let's make some music! Scales, as already discussed, tend to get a bad rap from students new to the guitar as they can seem very divorced from rock & roll. Yet once you have a few shapes under your belt you'll be amazed at what you can produce with a bit of imagination. Here I have written a couple of generic—almost clichéd—major and minor scale melodic instrumentals in order to demonstrate their musical qualities very clearly.

Important note: I have included these transcriptions here so you can see directly how the scales we've covered can be applied in a

"real music" situation—but as these include a fair amount of quite developed phrasing techniques, you may wish to tackle them in their entirety once you have completed the main body of the book.

However, don't let that stop you from trying some of the lead/ melody lines now—just don't get too caught up in the phrasing minutiae: getting a general gist of how the scales have been transformed into genuine melodies is enough. When you have spent more time on your bending and vibrato then by all means come back to these again.

MAJOR SCALE EXAMPLE—"TOP STEVE"

Named in homage to the woefully underrated Steve Stevens (an amazing six-stringer probably best known as Billy Idol's guitarist, but who also added his patented "stun guitar" to Michael Jackson's 1988 rock hit "Dirty Diana"), this is inspired by the main theme of *Top Gun*, on which Stevens contributed soaring lead guitar and melody lines. For the melodies I constructed a simple melodic tune that is played first of all below the twelfth fret using position five of the major scale. This is repeated and then the same basic melody is transposed an octave higher utilizing position 3.

Here's the complete transcription. There is a fair amount of bending and vibrato and it will take you a while to get this sounding authentic, but don't let that you stop you attempting the piece. If you're unsure of your pitching abilities, play the tune straight: i.e., instead of bending up to the notes, simply play the target note normally. This will require more lateral hand movement up and down the neck, but it will enable you to play the tune authentically if you're unsure of your ability to play in tune.

TRACKS
83 + 84

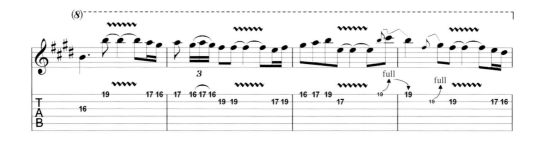

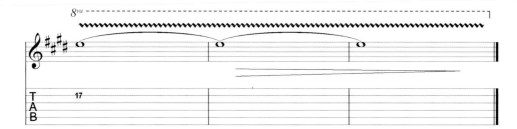

MINOR SCALE EXAMPLE—"GARY'S EUROPA"

This is a rock ballad in the style of Carlos Santana's classic 1975 track "Europa" to which I've also added a hint of the renowned Irish solo artist and ex-Thin Lizzy axman Gary Moore into the mix. This places a great deal of emphasis on soaring, emotion-drenched guitar work rather than speed. If you're not familiar with Gary Moore, check out songs such as "Parisienne Walkways," "Empty Rooms," "The Loner," "When The Messiah Comes," and "Still Got The Blues" amongst a ton of others—and get ready to make that ax weep.

Like "Top Steve," this is based around a simple tune that is first played below the twelfth fret, using position one of the B minor scale as the basis. This is then repeated and expanded upon above the twelfth fret.

There is more lateral movement in this track than "Top Steve," so don't be surprised if this takes a lot longer to learn. Here's the transcription: bending and vibrato are the key to making this sound effective.

TRACKS
85+86

CHAPTER NINE:
WHAT'S BEEN GOING ON?

This chapter is designed to give you a quick spin through the basics of some music theory. These are things which will help you on a day-to-day basis, rather than theory you need to pass a music exam. If you know a bit about how chords, scales, and arpeggios are constructed, as well as what keys are, it will really help you in your journey to becoming a rock god. Knowing this theory will really help when the time comes to jam and someone says "OK, let's just jam in A" or "Let's try a ballad in E minor."

THE FATHER OF MUSIC
THE MAJOR SCALE

The most important tool in music is the major scale. This group of notes forms the foundations of how we build all those power chords, chords, scales, and arpeggios we've encountered so far.

To recap: there are twelve notes in Western music:

A A♯/B♭ B C C♯/D♭ D D♯/E♭ E F F♯/G♭ G G♯/A♭

From each of these twelve starting notes, we can construct a major scale. All twelve major scales have the same internal construction, created by a set formula of "intervals" (an interval is the musical distance between any two notes).

In Western music the basic intervals are a "whole step" (marked as "W" below) and "half step" ("H"). On the fretboard, a whole step equates to two frets, and a half step is one fret. Let's jump in at the deep end and construct a couple of major scales.

EXAMPLE ONE: E MAJOR SCALE

Starting from E, those twelve notes in music are thus:

E F F♯/G♭ G G♯/A♭ A A♯/B♭ B C C♯/D♭ D D♯/E♭

Now try to construct an E major scale laterally on one string—it will be easier this way, trust me!

Apply the following structure:

```
1   2   3   4   5   6   7   1
  W   W   H   W   W   W   H
```

Add in the notes and you will get:

```
1   2   3   4   5   6   7   1
E   F♯  G♯  A   B   C♯  D♯  E
```

Played laterally on the sixth/low E string you will thus get:

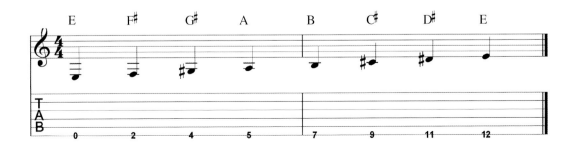

You can test this by trying any of the major scale shapes we looked at in Chapter Eight, starting from E, and seeing if the notes correspond. For example, here's the position four shape:

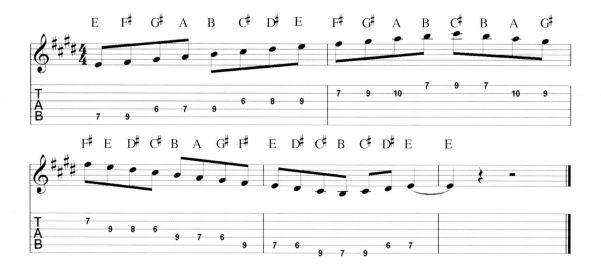

EXAMPLE TWO: C MAJOR SCALE

Now let's try another major scale to see if this all holds true.
Starting from C, those twelve notes in music are thus:

C C♯/D♭ D D♯/E♭ E F F♯/G♭ G G♯/A♭ A A♯/B♭ B

Again, construct a C major scale laterally on one string—the fifth/A string makes sense here.

Apply the following structure:

1   2   3   4   5   6   7   1
  W   W   H   W   W   W   H

Add in the notes and you will get:

1   2   3   4   5   6   7   1
C   D   E   F   G   A   B   C

Played laterally on the fifth/A string you will thus get:

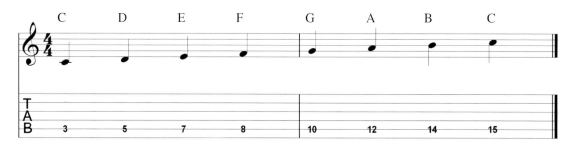

Here is a C major scale played using position 1:

MAJOR CHORDS

All basic major chords simply have the first, third, and fifth of the relevant major scale's notes played together.

EXAMPLE: G MAJOR

If you play a G major scale, you'll get the following notes:

G	A	B	C	D	E	F#	G
1	2	3	4	5	6	7	1

Stack the first, third, and fifth together and you'll get the following notes:

G	B	D
1	3	5

Play these together on the guitar in a couple of common G major shapes and you'll get:

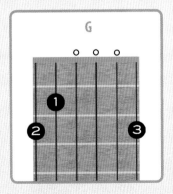

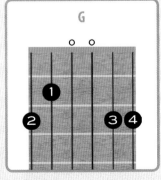

"But that's got six notes," I hear you cry: well, it may have six notes, but only three are actual different notes: this is because the note G is duplicated on the third fret of the sixth/low E, open on the third/G and again at the third fret of the first/top E strings—they are just in different octaves.

Shape 1 also has two B notes, at the second fret of the fifth/A string and the open one at the second/B string, and a single D note at the open fourth/D string. The second shape makes do with only one B note (at the second fret of the fifth/A string) but doubles up on the Ds, at the open fourth/D plus third fret string and another at the third fret of the second/B string.

EXAMPLE: C MAJOR

To illustrate this further, let's make another chord—C major. Again, start off by playing the relevant major scale:

C	D	E	F	G	A	B	C
1	2	3	4	5	6	7	1

Stack the first, third, and fifth together and you'll get the following notes:

C	E	G
1	3	5

Play these together on the guitar (shown here in the most commonly used open C major chord shape) and you'll get:

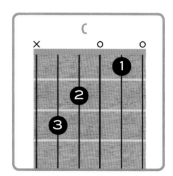

"But that one's got five notes," you might be thinking. As with the last example, it has in fact got three actual different notes. Here we have two Cs (third fret of the fifth/A string and first fret of the second/B string), a couple of Es (second fret fourth/D and open first/top E string), and a final G played open on the third/G string.

The same principle holds true for all basic major chords. Now let's see how we create minor chords.

MINOR CHORDS

All basic major chords simply have the first, third, and fifth of the relevant major scale's notes played together. All basic minor chords share the same first and fifth notes of the relevant major scale, but the third note (3) is flattened (♭3) to create that sad minor tonality much loved by rock ballads and metal guitarists. Let's construct a Dm chord to reinforce all of this.

EXAMPLE: D MINOR

Again, start off with the major scale to get your basic framework:

D major scale:

D	E	F♯	G	A	B	C♯
1	2	3	4	5	6	7

Stack the first, the ♭3, and the fifth together, and you'll get the following notes:

D	F	A
1	♭3	5

Hey presto: a D minor chord!

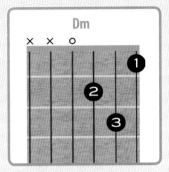

We don't need to go through all that depiction of notes business here do we? Suffice to say, there are only three separate notes here.

POWER CHORDS

A power chord is simply two notes stacked on top of each other and played at the same time. However, maybe you've noticed, looking back at all the riffs we've covered, that they're all called fifths—why is that? Well, a power chord is actually a simplified version of—for example—a plain old major or minor chord, but with the third removed. As we already noted in Chapter Five, its origins lie in the introduction of distortion to guitar players' tones back in the 1960s. Guitarists found that when playing the hitherto conventional chord shapes with distortion they could be too messy or busy-sounding. Hence the practice of removing the third from chords was established.

E major contains the notes:

E G♯ B
1 3   5

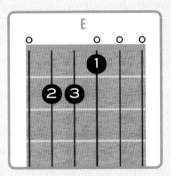

If you omit the third (G♯) you end up with simply a 1 (E) and a 5 (B). This still sounds, and functions, as an E-based chord, but has been simplified. Thus we arrive at power chord—literally a root (1) "E" and a fifth (5) "B"—hence the name "fifth."

E5 contains the notes:

E   B
1   5

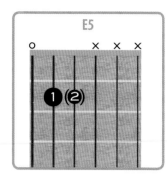

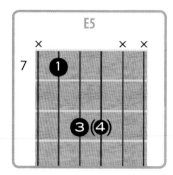

This works very well with distortion, and is a great device to use when you want some of that rock power in your songs.

SCALES

In this book we are dealing mainly with these four basic scale types:

- minor pentatonic
- minor blues scale
- major scale
- minor scale

We've already covered the major scale a few pages back so let's jump straight in and construct a few of these other dudes.

MINOR PENTATONIC

The basis of tons of music—and loads of guitar riffs, licks, and solos because the position one shape is so comfortable to play—this is simply a major scale with a couple of notes omitted and another couple altered.

Let's construct every rock and blues guitarist's old favorite, the A minor pentatonic.

As always, start with the major scale:

A   B   C♯   D   E   F♯   G♯
1   2   3   4   5   6   7

A minor pentatonic has the formula:

1   ♭3   4   5   ♭7

Apply this to the A major scale and we arrive at:

A   C   D   E   G
1   ♭3   4   5   ♭7

MINOR BLUES

A six-note derivation of the minor pentatonic, this simply adds in a ♭5 to create a cool bluesy feel—or if a different mood is required, plain evil…. Metal bands such as Black Sabbath and Metallica often use this as a basis for their riffs. Let's look at how they are created.

Let's do this in D.

D	E	F♯	G	A	B	C♯
1	2	3	4	5	6	7

The minor blues has the formula:

1	♭3	4	♭5	5	♭7

So D minor blues is:

D	F	G	A♭	A	C
1	♭3	4	♭5	5	♭7

THE NATURAL MINOR SCALE

Often referred to as the plain old minor scale, this is a real favorite for ballads and metal, so let's construct that favorite of all the metal bands—the E minor scale. As you know by now, we have to start with the major scale, so here it is in E:

E	F♯	G♯	A	B	C♯	D♯
1	2	3	4	5	6	7

The minor scale has the formula:

1	2	♭3	4	5	♭6	♭7

So the E minor scale is:

E	F♯	G	A	B	C	D
1	2	♭3	4	5	♭6	♭7

Now you know how chords and scales are constructed you are free to shout out "Why do I need to know all of this? I just want to rock!"

Let's imagine you come up with this great chord or riff and you want to know what to play over it or alongside it: sure, you can try to use your ears and stumble around until you find something that works—or you can analyze it super quickly with this basic knowledge and see what options you have straight away, knowing that they will all sound pretty cool.

It simply makes the whole creative process far quicker and easier—and the more you get into this stuff the more you realize that loads of famous songs all follow very similar rules or structures (similar riffs, scales, and chords for example) so if you know the tricks of the trade that your fave guitarists and bands all apply, you can use them yourself: remember, knowledge is power!

One very, very useful tool to have is a basic knowledge of keys, as almost all songs are based—at least in part—upon these (even if sometimes the composers aren't consciously aware of it themselves!). You've already been using keys throughout the book—now look at how they are created.

KEYS

Songs are often said to be "in the key of…"—and we've already discussed keys on a number of occasions throughout this book. But what are they? For the purposes of this book we are just going to look at keys from a pretty basic chordal perspective. Getting a good working knowledge of this will really aid your ability to work songs out, as well as helping you to come up with some cool stuff of your own.

The easiest way to describe a key is simply to construct one—so let's look at the key of A major first. Guess what—yes, keys are built from our good old buddy the major scale, so let us again play an A major scale to get us started:

A   B   C#   D   E   F#   G#

Now we will construct seven chords from each note.

Chords are built using stacked thirds—or tertiary construction, to be flashy with our terminology! What this basically means is that you leapfrog over adjacent notes to create the basic chords, as shown below:

I   A   B   C#   D   E   F#   G#   A

A C# E—not surprisingly this is A major.

You don't have to stop here with only three notes—if you wish you can stack other notes on top of these basic three notes, but for the purposes of this book we don't need to go into that. Just be aware that the option is there…

Now we start the same process from the second note…

II   A   B   C#   D   E   F#   G#   A

B D F#—played together these produce a B minor chord.

III   A   B   C#   D   E   F#   G#   A

C# E G#—played together these produce a C# minor chord.

IV   A   B   C#   D   E   F#   G#   A

D F# A—played together these produce a D major chord.

V   A   B   C#   D   E   F#   G#   A   B

E G# B—played together these produce an E major chord.

VI   A   B   C#   D   E   F#   G#   A   B   C#

F# A C#—played together these produce an F# minor chord.

VII A B C♯ D E F♯ G♯ A B C♯ D

G♯ B D—played together these produce a G# diminished chord.

Flip back to "Mad Thing" in Chapter Four where all these chords are displayed. Try playing them in succession, both ascending—i.e., A–Bm–C♯m, etc.—and descending, i.e., A–G♯dim–F♯m, etc.—to get a feel for the sound they make as a group.

I can already imagine you thinking "That last one sure sounds weird!" And you are right—it can be a tricky chord to deal with, which is why so many songwriters tend to either ignore it or substitute another chord in its place.

Two common substitutions are:

1) Flatten the VII chord and turn it into a major—much beloved of classic rockers the world over.
In this case you would simply play a G major, which has the notes G B D.

"But isn't that G wrong?" I hear you cry… Yes, technically it is, but it's a fine example of bending the rules—if it sounds good, it *is* good!

2) Turn the VII chord into a slash chord—in this case play the V chord and play the root note of the VII as the base note. This keeps the melodic contour of the scale/key intact, but provides an easier-sounding chord.
In this case you would play an E major with a G♯ in the base—which is written as E/G♯.

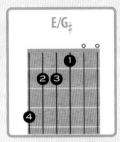
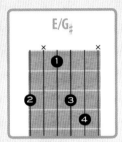

WHAT'S A SLASH CHORD?

We've already looked at some commonly used slash chords in Chapters Four and Five, and the simplest explanation is that it is a chord which has a note other than the root as its lowest note.

Common open slash chords include:

G/B   D/F♯

These are very common in acoustic guitar parts and those quiet song intros as well as being an integral part of many riffs from bands such as AC/DC, Queen, and Bad Company—y'know, classic rock stuff!

Common "triad"-based slash chords include:

D/A   G/A   E/A

These are integral to classic rock as well as much of the 1980s rock from bands such as Van Halen, Ratt, Poison, and Dokken—as well as the aforementioned classic rock monsters.

WHY IS KNOWING KEYS USEFUL?

Simply because a lot of rock classics are mainly key-based—so if you have a working knowledge of the most popularly used keys in guitar music, and have already got the physical aspects of these lodged in the old gray matter (i.e., you are used to the chord changes), you are one step ahead of the game when the time comes to learn how to play some of these classics.

It is worth noting—as you might have already guessed having worked through all those riffs in Chapters Four and Five—that most songs only actually utilize a few of the available chords within any key. It's a question of cherry picking the chords and mucking around until you come up with something that sounds hot!

Below is a diagram showing the most commonly used major keys in rock.

MAJOR KEYS

KEY	I	II	III	IV	V	VI	VII
A	A	Bm	C♯m	D	E	F♯m	G♯dim or E/G♯
C	C	Dm	Em	F	G	Am	B dim or G/B
D	D	Em	F♯m	G	A	Bm	C♯dim or A/C♯
F	F	F♯m	G♯m	A	B	C♯m	D♯dim or B/D♯
G	G	Am	Bm	C	D	Em	F♯dim or D/F♯

MINOR KEYS

A minor key is based upon the same principle as major keys—you pick your key, build a minor scale from the root note and harmonize it to build your seven basic chord types and you are away!

MINOR KEYS

KEY	I	II	III	IV	V	VI	VII
Am	Am	Bdim or G/B	C	Dm	Em	GF	G
Bm	Bm	C♯dim or A/C	D	Em	F♯m	G	A
C♯m	C♯m	D♯dim or B/C♯	E	F♯m	G♯m	A	B
Dm	Dm	Edim or C/E	F	Gm	Am	B♭	C
Em	Em	F♯dim or D/F♯	G	Am	Bm	C	D
F♯m	F♯m	G♯dim or E/G♯	A	Bm	C♯m	D	E
Gm	Gm	Adim or F/A	B♭	Cm	Dm	E♭	F

THE THEORY OF RELATIVITY...

Now, the most observant among you may may have realized that there are parallels between the major and minor keys' chord sequences—what gives? It's just another example of how everything in music is a matter of perspective: the major keys we looked at were only major keys because we chose to use (as thousands of songwriters have done so throughout history) a major chord to base our musical journey—a minor key is simply the same process but choosing instead to make a minor chord our "captain" chord.

Choosing a major chord as your song's basis will result in a happier-sounding song: lots of party rock songs from bands such as Kiss, Van Halen, and Poison—as well as punk bands such as Green Day and Blink 182—are inherently major-based, while a lot of ballads and metal bands tend to be minor-based.

Put as plainly as possible, the sixth note of any major scale generates the "relative" minor scale. The notes involved are the same, but that tilting of the perspective totally changes the musical feel. Now, this is a very simplistic definition, and one your high school music teacher or classical musician might question—but it is true nonetheless.

If you want to have a go at writing a song of your own, you can pick what sort of feel you require, and then use the basic major or minor keys as your basis. Now, the whole point of musical creativity is to express your own unique ideas, so if you so desire by all means throw every so-called rule out—but the reason so many songs have become global successes is because they share many common traits, so being aware of these can only help, can't it?

Anyway, how we started on this topic was that some of the major keys and minor keys we've just looked at share exactly the same chords—and the reason is down to a musical concept called relative keys.

We don't need to go into detail in this book on the theoretical reasons about why relative keys exist (hell, if you've made it this far in one sitting you're doing well!), so let's just look at a couple of practical ways you can use knowledge of all this "key" stuff to your advantage in a quick and easy way.

Examine the following diagram that shows the most commonly used relative major and minor keys:

RELATIVE KEYS

A major is "relative" to F#m
Thus they share the same notes and chords

C major is "relative" to Am
Thus they share the same notes and chords

D major is "relative" to Bm
Thus they share the same notes and chords

E major is "relative" to C#m
Thus they share the same notes and chords

G major is "relative" to Em
Thus they share the same notes and chords

SONGWRITING TIPS

Knowing these basic keys can be a real help for when you start to write your own songs.

For example, you may have a cool riff that seems to be "sort of D-ish"—now what?

DECIDE IF THAT RIFF HAS A MAJOR OR MINOR "FEEL"

How? Use your ears! Is it basically upbeat and happy-ish or sad/gloomy? Then you can pick any of the other basic chord types from the key you've decided upon and experiment: combine them in any old order—or disregard them totally. Knowing this stuff simply gives you more knowledge and more choices.

For example you can pick a "minor" feel for your verses, before upping the ante to a major key for the choruses—this is used by loads of bands such as Boston, Journey, and Aerosmith right through to Bon Jovi and Nickelback. Or you can do the reverse… Keep steadfastly major for the whole of the song—as mentioned previously, bands such as Kiss, Van Halen Poison, Green Day, Blink 182, and Good Charlotte have often done this because of the goodtime "party" feel it results in.

Conversely, stick to a determined minor feel, which many ballads (such as "Nothing Else Matters" by Metallica) and metal bands indulge in—almost all the classic songs by Black Sabbath and Iron Maiden (to name but two) are steadfastly minor.

BREAK THE RULES!

You can write a song based on a couple of "correct" chords from a key of your choice and then throw a curveball into the proceedings by making the next two completely unrelated—or switch the chord types around, or make them all major—there are countless ways you can take this knowledge of what a key is and twist it to make it your own.

Left: Good Charlotte's songwriting relies on major keys for its upbeat feel

Rock guitarist plays licks from his knees

CHAPTER TEN:
MIXING IT UP

In this chapter we will steadily incorporate some more advanced playing techniques to your licks, mix up some scales, and introduce you to some of the flash guitar tricks that rock and metal players love. To further mix things up, I have deviated from the previous practice of demonstrating licks solely in the key of A minor, moving to the metal-friendly E minor—but as these are all transferable, you can shift them up and down the neck and into as many keys as you wish.

DOUBLE STOPS

A double stop is the act of playing two notes from a scale together rather than consecutively. These are great at providing a bit of grunt and dirt amid your more scale-based and single-note improvisational licks.

Using your index finger simply barre the second and third strings at the twelfth fret and pull them toward the floor rhythmically (thus slightly sharpening/raising the notes), then use a standard pull-off idea before ending some vibrato at the fourteenth fret of the fourth string.

TRACK
87.1

This takes the same idea but introduces a barre at the fourteenth fret of the second and third strings.

TRACK
87.2

This adds some slides up to the equation, using fourths on the second and third strings.

TRACK
87.3

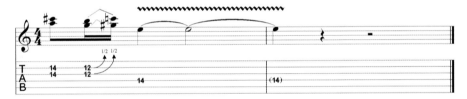

A Hendrix-style idea, where we use some hammer-ons and pull-offs to create a laidback lick that works equally well with distortion or a smooth front pick-up tone.

TRACK
87.4

UNISON BENDS

Jimi Hendrix utilized unison bends to great effect on the sublime "All Along The Watchtower," and players as varied as Carlos Santana and Zakk Wylde have made these a mainstay of their soloing.

Unison bends have the effect of really thickening the sound of bending notes, almost acting as a double tracking effect (double tracking being the term used to describe the recording technique of "doubling"—i.e., playing a phrase again and superimposing it on top of the original take). These will help your guitar sound much more substantial, and are a great device to use if you are the sole guitarist trying to beef up some melodies. While these are technically feasible on the thicker strings, you'd need Hulk-like strength to make them sound effective, so they are normally played on the second and third strings or the first and second.

UNISON WARRIORS

To hear these in action, check out the opening track of the CD, "The O Zone"—or Zakk Wylde's (pictured above) supercharged opening lines on Ozzy Osbourne's "Mr. Hyde."

These three exercises all look at unison bends utilizing the second and third strings. Fret a note on the second string with your index finger, then place your third finger two frets higher but on the third string. Make sure your second finger is tucked in behind the third finger to provide assistance. Play the two strings together and then, making sure both still ring clearly, push the third string up a whole step (i.e., 2 frets) until the pitches converge.

TRACK
◎
88.1.2.3

These exercises take the same principles but transfer them to the first and second strings. Notice that now you have to use a wider stretch—three frets rather than two—due to the larger difference in tuning intervals between the first and second strings. For this reason you may find these a bit trickier, although above the twelfth fret the difference really becomes negligible.

TRACK
◎
88.4.5.6

OCTAVES

Octaves are a common soloing technique used to add depth to simple melodies.

There's a multitude of ways these can be played on the guitar, but here we'll look at playing them via the fifth and third strings. These two strings provide the easiest way to execute octaves, as they don't require much of a fretting-hand stretch, and you should be fairly used to the basic shape as they are so closely linked to the power chords you already know.

The problems you will encounter with these relate to controlling the strings that are not actively involved. For octaves to work effectively you simply have to make sure that your index finger is on top of its game. Don't arch your fingers as if you are playing a chord, as that may cause the string in between the fretted notes (in the examples here specifically the fourth/D string) to ring out as the picking hand's role is solely in a strumming capacity, which means you can't rely on this to back you up for any muting duties.

Make sure that you are playing with a sufficient angle as well. You do not want these to be played with your fingers exactly parallel to the frets. This classical guitar hand position accentuates the tendency to arch your finger. If you need a reminder, go back to Chapter Two and check out the sections on fretting-hand positions.

Looking at this you can see the index finger has a lot to deal with—its underside muting the first, second, and fourth strings, but also stopping the sixth string by having the fingertip stubbing against it… it's enough to give you a migraine! Don't worry though, it does become instinctive.

This simply takes the notes D to E to G to A to B and plays them as straight octaves.

TRACK
89.1

Here we have the same notes, but played with a bit of a cooler rhythm as well as sliding between them.

TRACK
89.2

SCALE SEQUENCING

These are really cool ways to spice up all those scales we've been looking at. Metal guitarists in particular love using long minor scale sequences, often played at superhuman velocities with earthquake-inducing amounts of gain and attitude.

Sequencing can turn a mundane scale into a musical tool that sounds great in a multitude of musical situations. They are based upon the simple principle of establishing a basic musical pattern or "sequence" and replicating it, either ascending or descending, throughout the scale. They are particularly good for linking licks: often guitarists know a bunch of cool licks but don't necessarily know how to connect them all into a cohesive solo. They'll kick off with their favorite cool lick, but then noodle for a while through a scale until they find a moment that they can try and stun the audience with their next crowd-pleasing lick.

Having a bunch of cool scale sequences under your belt means that with a bit of thought, you can still base your solos on that same bunch of separate licks, but by linking them together with some cool scale sequences you can trick the audience into thinking you actually know what you are doing! With time and a bit of luck, you'll find that your solos begin to sound like you are making a valid musical statement instead of just noodling through a bunch of unconnected licks with only a meandering scale to act as the musical glue.

E MINOR PENTATONIC SEQUENCING LICK 1

This is a very basic descending idea where you simply repeat the two notes from each string of the minor pentatonic scale in a steady eighth-note rhythm. Here I have simply established the pattern on the first string and continued down the scale until the fourth string. Obviously you can continue until you run out of strings, should you so desire.

TRACK
90.1

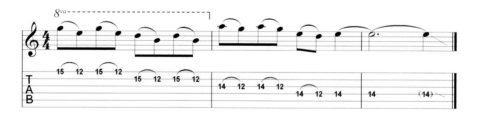

This is played utilizing pull-offs, but try playing this—and all the others—using strict alternate picking. Not only will they make excellent picking and left/right hand coordination exercises, but once you can increase the speed you'll be on the way to replicating the sound of renowned pentatonic pickers such as Ozzy Osbourne's (and Black Label Society's) main man, Zakk Wylde. Played as notated, but sped up massively, this is the sort of thing Thin Lizzy's guitarists used to enjoy playing.

E MINOR PENTATONIC SEQUENCING LICK 2

This takes the same eighth-note rhythm and ideas as the previous lick, but on beats 2 and 4 flips the pattern around and ascends back up the scale, so there's more picking to be dealt with. As with all of these sequencing ideas, check it out first on the CD so you get a mental reference point of what's happening before trying to execute the lick. Otherwise you may find that you tie yourself up in all sorts of weird musical situations.

If in doubt, always count! As it's eighth notes, I trust you remember this is: 1&, 2&, 3&, 4&…

JIMMY PAGE-STYLE DESCENDING E MINOR PENTATONIC SEQUENCE

We've already covered this basic idea in Chapter Seven, but here we take the basic idea and simply shift it up to E minor.

JIMMY PAGE-STYLE ASCENDING E MINOR PENTATONIC SEQUENCE

Here's the same thing, but ascending. For some reason many people find this trickier than the descending version, despite the fact that for most people hammer-ons seem to be easier than pull-offs. Go figure…

TWISTY E MINOR PENTATONIC LICK

This is a cool idea that combines the last two licks into one "twisty" lick. An unusual and very smooth lick that will gain you many admirers!

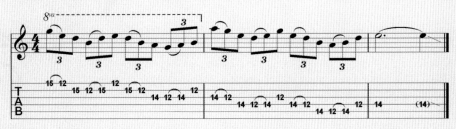

C MAJOR / A MINOR SCALE ASCENDING IN GROUPS OF FOUR

Ascending or descending scales in groups of four notes is a very common technique based on classical compositional ideas. Players such as Ritchie Blackmore, Randy Rhoads, and Yngwie Malmsteen were pivotal in introducing these into the modern rock guitarist's vocabulary. This is a cool and relatively easy-to-apply lick that stays solely on the first string, thus taking some pressure off your picking hand. This works equally well over C or Am, so have fun! Make sure you apply strict alternate picking throughout.

TRACK
92.1

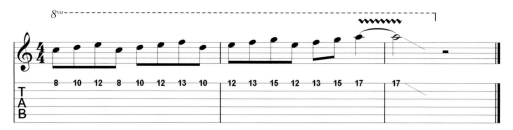

C MAJOR / A MINOR SCALE DESCENDING IN GROUPS OF FOUR

This descending sequence is trickier as it involves keeping strict alternate picking when playing the pattern through several strings. While this is equally feasible played just on the first string, the added tonal richness of the thicker second and third strings warrants the extra effort—particularly when it comes to applying the vibrato on that final A note.

TRACK
92.2

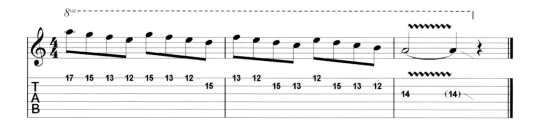

E MINOR ASCENDING IN SECONDS AND THIRDS

Another classically inspired sequence, this simply ascends through an E minor scale; again, watch for keeping the picking strictly alternate. As these examples are played at a comparatively slow tempo, it's quite easy just to down-pick everything—but that's a false economy as problems will arise when you need to speed this up: so be vigilant now!

E MINOR DESCENDING IN SECONDS AND THIRDS

More of the same, just descending.

SEQUENTIAL SUCCESS STORIES

The aforementioned guitarists—Ritchie Blackmore, Randy Rhoads, and Yngwie Malmsteen—are essential listening, as are Al DiMeola, Vinnie Moore, Paul Gilbert, and Tony Macalpine.

ARPEGGIOS

An arpeggio is simply the notes of a chord played individually. Once mainly ignored by rock guitarists, the classical influences that began to filter into rock and metal in the early 1970s meant that suddenly a whole generation of players embraced arpeggios.

By the late 1980s they were omnipresent, often played at warp speed and combining a multitude of exotic playing techniques such as sweep picking, string skipping, and even eight-finger tapping! However, we will simply take a brief look at arguably the simplest arpeggios to perform on the guitar, two-string major and minor triads.

MAJOR AND MINOR TRIADIC TWO-STRING ARPEGGIOS

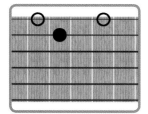

Major root second/B string

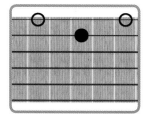

Minor root second/B string

The following exercise simply plays Em to D to C with the root notes on the second string. Experiment away and come up with some cool sequences to use in your own music.

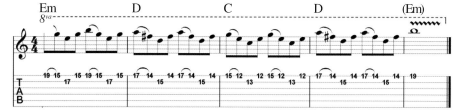

These are fairly straightforward to play, and at the tempo demonstrated on the CD, they are equally easy played with pull-offs as notated or by picking every note. The main consideration is not to let the notes bleed into each other.

ARTFUL ARPEGGIOS

Almost all of Ritchie Blackmore's work involves arpeggios to some degree or other, none more so than "Burn." Iron Maiden, Megadeth, and Metallica have all used two-string arpeggios. And no feature on arpeggios in a rock book can fail to mention Yngwie Malmsteen, who ripped into the rock guitar scene in 1983 and quite simply took things to a new level. Other players who have utilized arpeggios to a large degree include Jason Becker, Tony Macalpine, Vinnie Moore, Greg Howe, Marty Friedman, Paul Gilbert, and Richie Kotzen.

TAPPING TIME

In 1978 Eddie Van Halen revolutionized guitar playing with his "two-handed tapping" technique, most famously demonstrated on the track "Eruption," from Van Halen's 1978 self-titled debut album.

Tapping is based on the simple concept of using the picking hand to reach over the fretboard and "tap," using hammer-ons and pull-offs, notes that would have been previously out of reach if utilizing "conventional" fretting-hand techniques. In essence, using the picking hand's fingers to sound notes higher up the fretboard enabled guitarists to play previously impossible licks due to the constraints imposed by the size and reach of the human hand.

Before Van Halen, a few guitarists had flirted with this technique—noticeably ZZ Top's Billy Gibbons and Genesis' Steve Hackett—but no one had ever made the guitar sound like Eddie!

A MINOR TAPPING STUDY 1

A lot of basic tapping ideas are built around arpeggios: the large intervals between the notes are ideal to be played with using two-handed tapping in a linear fashion along one string.

TRACK
93.2

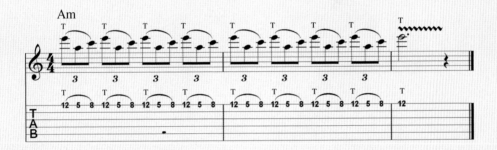

Firstly, you need to think about what finger to use to perform the tap. Eddie Van Halen uses his index finger, whereas in an example like this one Steve Vai, for example, would use his middle finger. I would advise that you get used to the latter: that way you don't have to worry so much about what to do with the pick. Secondly, make sure the tapping motion is strong enough: imagine you are trying to push the string through the wood of the fretboard! It helps to be placed right over the fret you are going to tap so that all your motion is in one powerful direction.

Thirdly, you have to actually perform a pull-off, not a lift-off. A lot of people new to tapping peck at the strings like an irritated woodpecker. Perform the basic movement at a moderate pace, making sure you're playing with sufficient attack and positivity.

Now you need to consider, when you pull off with your tapping finger, do you go downward toward the floor, or upward, almost curling your finger into your palm area? Both techniques have their advantages. I tend to pull upward as it seems to aid muting, but it depends on the lick. Many players achieve mind-blowing results using either method, so experiment.

You may have noticed that dreaded word "muting" cropping up again in the last paragraph. I'm afraid that, even though we're doing something cool and exotic, it doesn't mean that you can relax your vigilance over muting—in fact, all that shuffling around over the fretboard can actually increase the likelihood of errant string noise!

TAPPING STUDY 2: MOVING THE TAP

This takes the same basic idea but just expands the melody by moving the tapped notes while keeping the fretting hand constant.

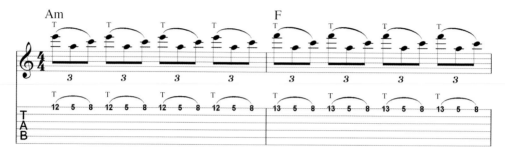

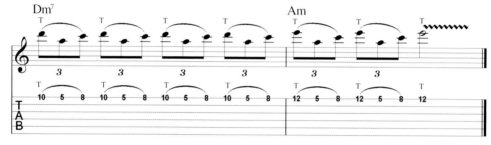

TAPPING STUDY 3: MOVING THE FRETTING HAND

Now let's reverse the process by keeping the tapped note constant but moving the fretting hand's notes.

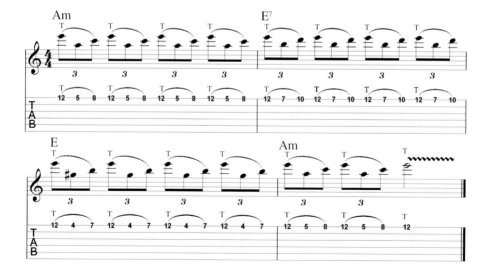

TWO-STRING TAPPING ETUDE

Finally, having based ourselves on purely on the first string, let's expand this by including the second string. This exercise is simple enough to remember as the shapes are simply shifted over from string to string—but you may find some of this tricky due to the fretting hand's stretch. Stick with it…

TRACK
◎
93.5

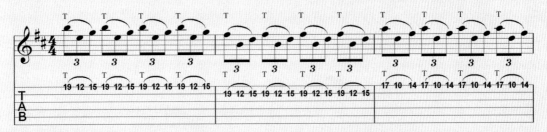

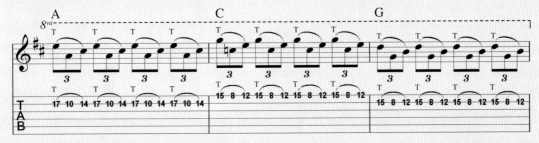

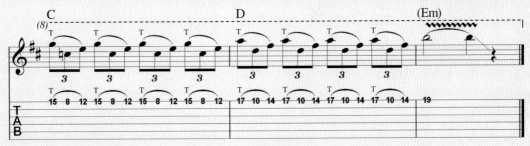

TOP TAPSTERS

Obviously Eddie Van Halen is essential! You may also wish to check out Steve Vai and Joe Satriani; and Greg Howe, Richie Kotzen, Nuno Bettancourt, and Reb Beach: all renowned masters of the tap.

If you want to be really freaked out, check out some of the super-advanced "eight-finger" tapping by players such as Jennifer Batten, TJ Helmerich, Bumblefoot, Guthrie Govan, and Buckethead as well as a new generation of players such as Megadeth guitarist Chris Broderick and Guitar Idol star Daniel Gottardo.

HARMONICS

Harmonics have been a staple of many guitarists' style for decades, but it was only really in the 1970s that rock guitarists started playing them with real gusto.

ZZ Top's Billy Gibbons was particularly partial to these, but it was really Eddie Van Halen's ripping up of the rulebook that established harmonics as an essential part of the rock guitarist's vocabulary.

Harmonics on the guitar are found on each string all over the neck, and there are several ways to generate them. We will look at the simplest: standard natural harmonics, generated by lightly touching a string directly over the fret itself—i.e., the metal—as opposed to the conventional means of generating a note by fretting down the string in the gaps between the frets. Played accurately, this technique generates a very "pure" sound that is quite different in tone to a standard note. These harmonics are generated by points on the strings known as "nodes" and you need to be very accurate with the finger placement to generate them. Use the smallest possible surface area of your fingertip. Once you've picked the note, remove your finger from the string and you should find it still vibrates, creating the harmonic.

The primary nodes are found at the twelfth, seventh, and fifth frets, although the example in this section also utilizes the harmonics found at the fourth and ninth frets.

OPEN-STRING HARMONICS

This is a cool ascending lick that covers the twelfth-fret harmonics starting from the third string, moving to the first, then traversing the first string via the seventh and fifth frets—conversely going up in pitch. You may find all these examples easier to execute using your third or fourth fingers as their "fingerprint" is smaller due to being thinner than your stronger first and second fingers. Remember that strength is not required here—what you are after is finger placement accuracy.

TRACK
◎
94.1

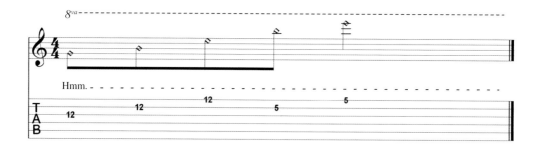

FIFTH-FRET OPEN-STRING HARMONICS

Here we're just sticking in one area of the neck, concentrating on the trickier-to-execute fifth-fret harmonics. You'll have to strive to keep your "fingerprint" as small as possible so you don't blunt the vibrations of the strings, and remember to lift off once you've achieved a sound harmonic note.

You should find that the twelfth-fret harmonics are fairly easy to master, but they get progressively trickier to play as you travel toward the nut. Also, you will find it easier to generate a powerful harmonic with the thicker strings, as they have more mass than the thinner treble strings, and you don't need to be quite as accurate in being exactly over the fret.

TRACK
94.2

In all these exercises it is worth noting that moving a fraction of an inch either way can make all the difference, so if something sounds clunky, you've probably drifted away from being over the fret, or are simply leaving your finger down for too long on a string and restricting its vibration. It can be a fine line to master this: take your finger off too quickly and you risk not attaining the note; too slowly and it will blunt the effect.

Concentrate and stick with it, though, and you will gain an instinctive feel for this technique. Don't ignore harmonics if they don't become easy immediately: they are an endlessly fascinating way to spice up previously mundane riffs and licks. Here are a couple of cool harmonics-based licks which you should be able to apply pretty quickly.

EDDIE VAN HALEN OPEN HARMONICS LICK IN E

This is great to play over an E major—or E5—chord.

TRACK
94.3

EDDIE VAN HALEN OPEN HARMONICS LICK IN A

Move the same pattern to the next three strings and we have something that is great over an A major, or—you guessed it!—A5 chord.

TRACK
94.4

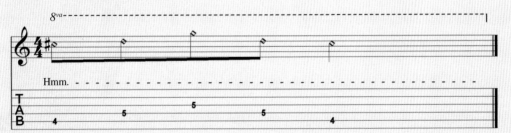

Both of these are very much in the style of Eddie Van Halen and Brad Gillis, who used to take these basic harmonic licks and add in a dose of whammy bar trickery—more of which in a couple of pages!

TREMOLO PICKING

For a perfect example of tremolo picking in a rock context, check out the climax of Eddie Van Halen's solo in the Michael Jackson song "Beat It."

This picking technique is one of the few times when you can truly throw caution to the wind, not worry too much about perfect left/right-hand synchronicity, and simply pick like hell! The basic concept is to sort out a cool scale sequence of notes and just go for it—basically picking as fast as you can using alternate picking. This is definitely not one for just using down-picks!

ASCENDING TREMOLO PICKING (FIRST STRING)

This is great to play over an E power chord.

TRACK
94.5

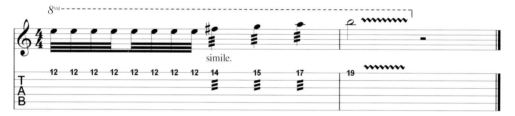

A simple enough idea, taking an E minor scale and going for it purely on the first string, which means that you don't have any string changes to deal with.

ASCENDING TREMOLO PICKING (SECOND AND THIRD STRINGS)

This is a longer sequence utilizing the same scale, but this time starting on the third string, then shifting to the second.

TRACK
94.6

WHAMMY BAR WILDNESS

Jimi Hendrix and Jeff Beck both started using the whammy bar in earnest in the mid-to-late 1960s, but for most rock and metal players the reference points are Eddie Van Halen, Steve Vai, and Joe Satriani.

Eddie started off using a stock Fender Stratocaster tremolo system, but quickly hooked up with Floyd Rose who had developed a double-locking system that clamped the strings with a vise-like grip enabling previously unfeasible expression and tuning stability. Thus a whole new vocabulary was available and guitarists soon jumped on it—particularly rock and metal players.

These whammy bar examples are designed to give you a quick fix in this technique. Subtle they are not; by the time you get all sophisticated and are trying to incorporate tasteful whammy bar licks, you will probably have had a whole lot longer playing the guitar and your natural aptitude will have developed. In all these examples you may wonder what to do about muting. You'll note that the physical act of grabbing that whammy bar takes your picking hand away from the main body of the strings, thus taking away a massive level of control. The answer? Don't worry about it! I know this seems opposite advice to everything we've established as correct technique, but bear with me: most of these examples are used as sonic effects so any errant strings being sounded actually add to the wild sounds we're going for here.

These examples are all played with a Floyd Rose-equipped guitar and are fairly extreme, so if you have a standard trem-equipped guitar, approach them with caution!

LOW E DIVEBOMB

As simple as it gets really—hit the sixth/low E string open, push the bar down to slack, and let the spring tension of the tremolo system bring the string back to normal.

TRACK
94.7

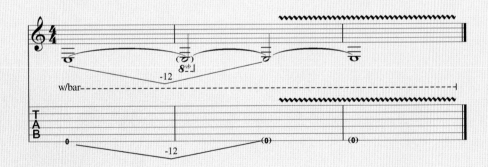

NINTH FRET THIRD STRING HARMONIC DIVEBOMB

Now let's apply harmonics to our whammy bar licks. Harmonics and the whammy bar are natural bedfellows: their uniquely pure tonal characteristics react amazingly well with the extreme pitch manipulation that the whammy provides—so have fun!

   This is simple enough: hit the harmonic clearly on the third string and depress the bar like hell. Sure, you can attain the exact same sound on the second or first strings, but the G string is the coolest as it goes slack whilst maintaining a clearly defined sound better than the thinner strings.

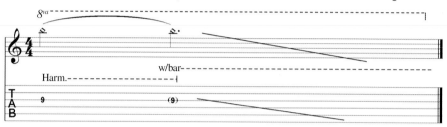

STEVE VAI-STYLE HARMONIC WHAMMY BAR LICK

When Dave Lee Roth left Van Halen in 1984, the guitar world was eager to see who could replace Eddie as Dave's six-string compadre. Ex-Frank Zappa wunderkind Steve Vai did not disappoint, bringing to the musical feast a sort of "Eddie Van Halen on steroids" approach.

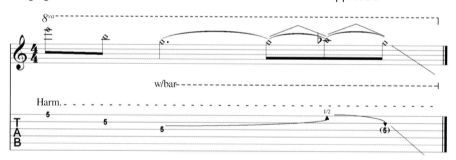

This lick simply takes the fifth-fret open harmonics from the first, second, and third strings and adds a healthy dose of whammy vibrato to the equation, finishing up with a divebomb.

STEVE VAI-STYLE SCOOP WHAMMY BAR LICK

Finally, let's look at a scooping lick. Scooping is when you depress the bar before playing a note and bring the bar back to a neutral position. Here we add some whammy bar vibrato to complete the lick.

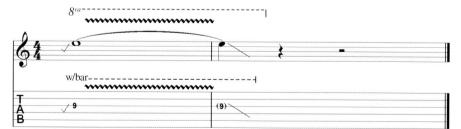

RED-HOT LICKS & RUNS

RED-HOT LICKS & RUNS 1

This one is simple enough: fret the fifteenth fret of the second string with your third finger at the same time as fretting the fourteenth fret of the third string with your second finger. Back that second finger up with your index finger, push the string up a whole step (two frets), and shake like hell! This sounds great with the whammy bar or using finger vibrato.

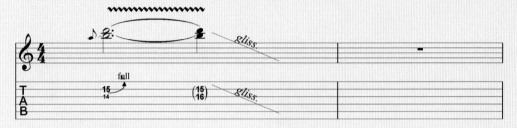

RED-HOT LICKS & RUNS 2

A repetition-style lick, this is based on repeating a four-note descending pattern from the E minor blues scale. No more and no less: for an example in A, played at hyper speed, check out the second section of Van Halen's "Eruption."

Nuno Bettencourt, of Boston-based rockers Extreme, utilizes something very similar—using the E minor blues scale—on their hit "Get The Funk Out." Ax-slinger Doug Aldrich (Bad Moon Rising, Dio, Whitesnake) is simply brilliant at this sort of repetitive lick.

RED-HOT LICKS & RUNS 3

Another repetitive lick utilizing the unique tonal qualities of the blues scale, this is more like the sort of thing George Lynch or Warren DeMartini might incorporate.

RED-HOT LICKS & RUNS 4

In this more traditional lick, we are combining the E minor scale's second note (F#) with a stock pentatonic phrase. Think Michael Shenker.

TRACK
95.3

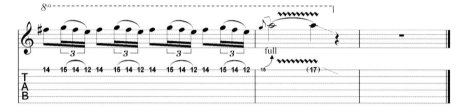

RED-HOT LICKS & RUNS 5

Another repetitive lick, this one takes the same pattern established with lick 3 but simply transfers it onto the first string, thus bringing the second note into play.

TRACK
95.4

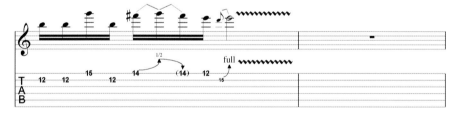

RED-HOT LICKS & RUNS 6

Using the twelfth fret of the second string as a basis, this creates a melodic pattern by alternately bouncing off the fifteenth and fourteenth frets of the first string. Again, this has shades of Mr. Shenker.

TRACK
95.5

RED-HOT LICKS & RUNS 7

A scale sequence using the full E minor scale (E, F#, G, A, B, C, D), this is a great little ditty which, when it's sped up, adds the perfect climax to a classic metal solo. Use strict alternate picking and the front/neck pick-up to really nail the tone.

TRACK
95.7

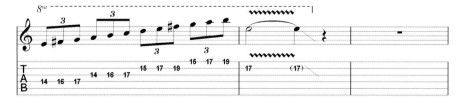

RED-HOT LICKS & RUNS 8

Here's a lengthy legato idea similar to the sort of runs which George Lynch made his own, as well as Iron Maiden's Dave Murray. Like the last lick, one this uses the E minor scale. The main technical consideration is ensuring an evenness of tone and consistent attack, but we are solely using hammer-ons, which are easier to execute than pull-offs, so this should be fairly approachable. When played at warp speed this sort of lick provides a fantastic sense of excitement and release at the climax of a solo—but be aware that this sort of thing is mostly played at six notes per beat (our example is in triplets—an easier three notes per beat). This also makes for an excellent picking exercise, so try using alternate picking and pick every note as well.

TRACK

95.8

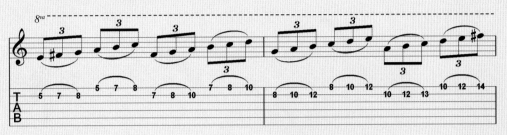

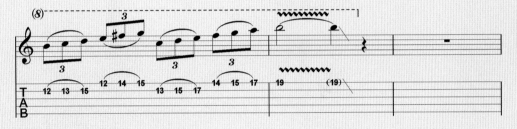

RED-HOT LICKS & RUNS 9

The final example looks at a similar E minor scale sequence and shape to the one we used in lick 7, but concentrates on a descending pattern. Again, use strict alternate picking and the front/neck pickup.

TRACK

95.9

Now we have some hot licks and runs sorted, the time comes to put these into practice, so turn the page and get ready to burn…

Concert crowd cheers
for the band

CHAPTER ELEVEN:
TIME TO BURN

We're now reaching the end of our rock guitar odyssey—and in this chapter the time has come to utilize all the rhythmic skills and licks we've covered, putting them into practice by coming up with your own solos and ideas over some cookin' backing tracks. There are also transcriptions of the rhythm guitar parts: as you are aware by now, it is equally important to develop a sound rhythm guitar ability as it is to be able to solo.

"WHEN BILLY MET GEORGE" SOLO

This a blowout over the ZZ Top-style groove in A that we utilized in Chapter Seven. It sounds like some freak combination of Billy Gibbons (ZZ Top, naturally) George Lynch, and even a hint of ol' Uncle Ted Nugent! So apologies for gratuitous lack of restraint and taste. Sometimes you've just got to throw caution to the wind and have a blast! This track really is something for you guys to aim for, so don't worry if some of this seems impossible. In time you should find it achievable as all the elements contained here are developments of ideas we've covered in this book—it's just that some are played at blazing speed!

TRACK
96

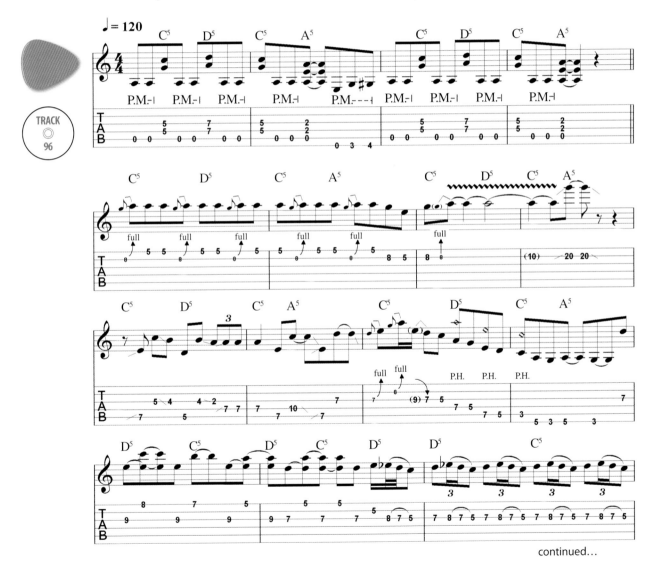

continued…

...continued

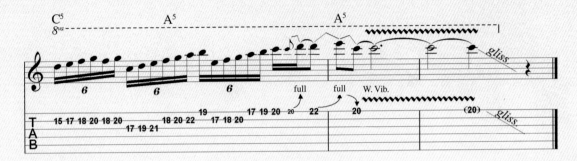

"WHEN BILLY MET GEORGE"—RHYTHM TRACK

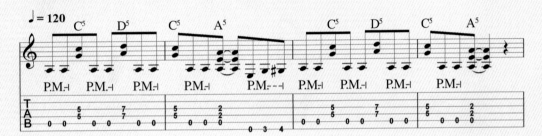

There's nothing too tricky here. it's mainly based on the sort of fourths we looked at in "Smokin' all Night Long" back in Chapter Five. On the CD you have the bass and drums to play along with—but if you need to isolate what the guitar's doing, flip back to Track 76 before attempting this.

"THE O ZONE"
BONUS RHYTHM TRACK

The intro track to this CD is a piece I came up with to demonstrate the sort of rock guitar playing that many of the artists and influences quoted in this book are famous for.

Being a showcase track, the solo parts are beyond the levels that this book has focused on—but don't let that stop you from ripping out your own version, and having a go at playing the rhythm parts, which we've transcribed below. Here is the track without the lead guitar parts so you can jam away until your fingers are bleedin' and raw.

The track is based on three sections. The main riff and secondary section are both suitable for you to improvise over, using a combination of the following:

E minor pentatonic (E G A B D E)
E minor blues scale (E G A B♭ B D E)
E minor scale (E F♯ G A B C D E)

You can also feel free to put in some C♯s and D♯s—but I'll leave that to your discretion. The third section modulates to A minor. Here you can just switch to the A minor-based scales we've already looked at for "When Billy Met George" as well as the full A minor scale. You can experiment in adding in some additional notes—F♯ works particularly well, giving a "dorian" flavor to the piece. Finally, the track ends with a repeat of the main riff, which means we're back in E territory.

...continued

WHAT NOW?

The goal of this book has been very simple: to get you a rock-solid (pun intended!) understanding of, and practical ability in, playing cool rock guitar as quickly as possible.

We've shed some standard teaching methods and concentrated on the core elements of rock guitar. Whether you started this book as a raw beginner or someone who's dabbled for weeks, months, or years, there is no doubt that you are in a much better place as a guitarist now than when you first purchased this book. The question you need to ask yourself now is "What next?" Is this all only for your private enjoyment—do you just want to have a blast rocking out at home? Or do you want to entertain in public? Whatever your aspirations, the way to achieving them is to identify them. Set some realistic short-term goals—and by that I mean months, not years! Follow this step-by-step guide to continued improvement and you're sure to start hitting those targets.

DEVISE A WEEKLY PROGRAM

This could be something along these lines:

DAY ONE—devise a practice schedule for the week, based upon the suggestions below. Write down what you practice today, recording any targets you've achieved.

DAY TWO—concentrate on something different. Write down what you've practiced.

DAY THREE—again move onto something new, still making sure you write down what you've covered.

DAY FOUR—cover the same material you practiced on Day One.

DAY FIVE—revisit Day Two's schedule.

DAY SIX—have another go at Day Three's schedule.

DAY SEVEN—anything goes! Just muck around and noodle away to your heart's content!

KEEP A PRACTICE DIARY

The secret to maintaining a regular and consistent practice schedule is enough variety to alleviate boredom setting in, but also to ensure that you thoroughly master the various exercises, techniques, riffs, and licks that will enable you to perform some cool songs.

To help make sure that you don't neglect any areas, keep a practice journal or diary. If working on technical exercises that require specific metronome targets always jot down the maximum tempo you've achieved—looking back weeks or months later you should be able to see a clear progression. Being able to quantify your increases in technical ability is a great motivational tool!

RECORD YOURSELF

Too often when we're learning we get so bogged down in the physical aspects of playing that we can forget to actually listen to what we're producing. What is needed is some distance—so record yourself when you think you've mastered a particular piece, then put it to one side for a few days. Come back to it with fresh ears and you will be able to assess much more clearly what the results are. The likelihood is that you'll instantly hear faults that need rectifying—but you may very well impress yourself!

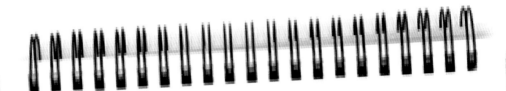

DAILY PRACTICE SCHEDULE

It is impossible to recommend a standard practice schedule that will suit everyone, but let's look at what should be achievable for most people: 90 minutes per day.

1) TECHNICAL WARM-UPS AND EXERCISES: 10 MINUTES
Pick a couple of exercises from Chapter Three and start slowly, at 60 bpm. Gradually increase the tempo on the metronome until you are comfortable at around 180 bpm.

2) RHYTHMIC WARM-UPS: 10 MINUTES
Again, pick a couple of exercises from Chapter Three and start slowly—maybe 60 bpm. Gradually increase the tempo on the metronome until you are comfortable at approximately 180 bpm.

3) RIFFS: 10 MINUTES
Pick a couple of riffs from any of Chapters Four to Six. When you have mastered these, try some new ones of your own from guitar magazines, books, or websites.

4) PHRASING TECHNIQUES: 10 MINUTES
Pick a couple of exercises from Chapter Seven.

5) SCALES: 10 MINUTES
Run through the scales from Chapter Eight with your metronome and gradually increase speed.

6) LICKS: 15 MINUTES
Pick a couple of licks from Chapter Seven as well as Chapter Ten.

7) IMPROVISING: 15 MINUTES
Play over the backing tracks from Chapters Seven, Eight, and Eleven. Have fun, rip it up, and just see what comes out.

8) ANYTHING GOES: 10 MINUTES
Come up with some of your own stuff—write some riffs, play along with a cool track, just muck around. At this point you should be thoroughly warmed up and "in tune" with the instrument, so now's the time to pull it all together.

RECOMMENDED LISTENING

This could be a neverending list, but there are definitely a few key players and bands whose playing you should make sure you check out. Whether you are determinedly in the classic rock and blues camp, or accept nothing less than bowel-scraping death metal, it's absolutely essential that you're aware of the following players:

ERIC CLAPTON (with Cream and as a solo artist)
JIMI HENDRIX (solo artist)
TONY IOMMI (with Black Sabbath)

JIMMY PAGE (with Led Zeppelin)
EDDIE VAN HALEN (with Van Halen)

The following bands and artists have all achieved International success and have all made a helped to further the art of rock guitar. You will notice a few bands and artists listed below are not strictly rockers—but they are included because their guitarists have been a major influence on countless rock and metal players… I shall leave you to decide who I'm talking about!

AC/DC (Malcolm and Angus Young)
AEROSMITH (Joe Perry, Brad Whitford)
THE ALLMAN BROTHERS (Duane Allman, Dickey Betts, Warren Hodges, Derek Trucks)
ANTHRAX (Scott Ian, Dan Spitz, Rob Caggiano)
AVENGED SEVENFOLD (Synyster Gates, Zacky Vengeance)
THE BEATLES (George Harrison)
JEFF BECK (solo artist)
BON JOVI (Richie Sambora)
BOSTON (Tom Scholz, Barry Goudreau, Gary Pihl)
DAVE LEE ROTH (Steve Vai, Jason Becker, John 5)
DEEP PURPLE (Ritchie Blackmore, Steve Morse)
DEF LEPPARD (Steve Clark, Phil Collen, Viv Campbell)
DIRE STRAITS (Mark Knopfler)
DOKKEN (George Lynch)
DREAM THEATER (John Petrucci)
EAGLES (Glenn Frey, Don Felder, Bernie Leadon, Joe Walsh, Steuart Smith)
EUROPE (John Norum, Kee Marcello)
GENESIS (Anthony Phillips, Steve Hackett, Mick Rutherford)
GUNS 'N' ROSES (Slash, Izzy Stradlin, Gilby Clarke, Robin Fincke, Buckethead, Bumblefoot)
IRON MAIDEN (Dave Murray, Dennis Stratton, Adrian Smith, Janick Gers)
ERIC JOHNSON (solo artist)
JOURNEY (Neal Schon)
JUDAS PRIEST (KK Downing, Glenn Tipton)
KILLSWITCH ENGAGE (Adam Dutkiewicz, Joel Stroetzel)
KISS (Ace Frehley, Paul Stanley, Vinnie Vincent, Mark St John, Bruce Kulick, Tommy Thayer)
KORN (James "Munky" Shaffer, Brian "Head" Welch)
LYNYRD SKYNYRD (Gary Rossington, Allen Collins, Ed King, Steve Gaines, Randall Hall, Rickey Medlocke)
MARILYN MANSON (Twiggy Ramirez, John 5)
MEGADETH (Dave Mustaine, Chris Poland, Jeff Young, Marty Friedman, Al Pitrelli, Glen Drover, Chris Broderick)
METALLICA (James Hetfield, Dave Mustaine, Kirk Hammet)
NIRVANA (Kurt Cobain)
OZZY OSBOURNE (Randy Rhoads, Bernie Torme, Brad Gillis, Jake E Lee, Joe Holmes, Zakk Wylde)
PANTERA (Dimebag Darrell)
PINK FLOYD (David Gilmour)
QUEEN (Brian May)
RAGE AGAINST THE MACHINE (Tom Morello)
RAINBOW (Ritchie Blackmore)
ROLLING STONES (Keith Richards, Brian Jones, Mick Taylor, Ronnie Wood)
RUSH (Alex Lifeson)
JOE SATRIANI (solo artist)
THE SCORPIONS (Uli John Roth, Michael Shenker, Rudolph Shenker, Matthias Jabs)
SLAYER (Jeff Hanneman, Kerry King)
SLIPKNOT (Mick Thomson, Jim Root)
THIN LIZZY (Eric Bell, Gary Moore, Brian Robertson, Scott Gorham, Snowy White, John Sykes)
TOTO (Steve Lukather)
UFO (Bernie Marsden, Michael Shenker, Paul Chapman, Atomik Tommy M, Laurence Archer, Vinnie Moore)
STEVE VAI (solo artist)
STEVIE RAY VAUGHAN (solo artist)
WHITESNAKE (Bernie Marsden, Micky Moody, John Sykes, Viv Campbell, Adrian Vandenburg, Steve Vai, Doug Aldrich, Reb Beach)
YES (Steve Howe, Trevor Rabin)
ZZ TOP (Billy Gibbons)

In addition make sure you check out the following amazing guitarists. None of these are household names but all are absolute masters of the guitar.

JENNIFER BATTEN www.jenniferbatten.com
SHAUN BAXTER www.myspace.com/shaunbaxter
JASON BECKER www.jasonbecker.com
THOMAS BLUG www.thomasblug.de / www.myspace.com/thomasblug
EDWARD BOX www.edwardbox.com / http://www.myspace.com/edwardbox
BUCKETHEAD www.bucketheadland.com
BUMBLEFOOT www.bumblefoot.com
DARIO CORTESE http://uk.myspace.com/dariocortese
WARREN DE MARTINI (Ratt) www.myspace.com/warren_demartini / www.therattpack.com
JOHN DENNER www.johndennerrocks.com
MATTHIAS IA EKLUNDH www.freakguitar.com
MICHAEL LEE FIRKINS www.michaelleefirkins.com / www.myspace.com/michaelleefirkins
MARTY FRIEDMAN www.martyfriedman.com
DERRYL GABEL www.myspace.com/derrylgabel
BRETT GARSED www.brettgarsed.com
PAUL GILBERT www.paulgilbert.com
DANIELE GOTTARDO www.danielegottardo.com/ www.myspace.com/danielegottardo
MARTIN GOULDING www.martingoulding.com
GUTHRIE GOVAN www.guthriegovan.co.uk / www.myspace.com/guthriegovaneroticcakes
TJ HELMERICH www.myspace.com/tjhelmerich
PHIL HILBORNE www.philhilborne.com / www.myspace.com/philhilborne
JOEL HOEKSTRA www.joelhoekstra.com / www.myspace.com/joelhoekstra
ALLAN HOLDSWORTH www.therealallanholdsworth.com
GREG HOWE www.greghowe.com
DAN HUFF www.myspace.com/gianttheband
JAMIE HUMPHRIES www.jamiehumphries.com / www.myspace.com/jamiehumphries
ANDY JAMES www.myspace.com/andyjamesf1
DAVE KILMINSTER www.davekilminster.com / www.myspace.com/davekilminster
JEFF KOLLMAN www.jeffkollman.com / www.myspace.com/jeffkollman
RICHIE KOTZEN www.richiekotzen.com
MICHAEL LANDAU www.mikelandau.com / www.myspace.com/michaellandau
SIMON LEES www.simonlees.co.uk
JEFF LOOMIS www.jeffloomis.com / www.myspace.com/jeffloomis
KIKO LOUREIRO www.kikoloureiro.com.br / www.myspace.com/kikoloureiroband
TONY MACALPINE www.tonymacalpine.com
ROB MARCELLO www.robertmarcello.net / www.myspace.com/dangerdangerrob
BERNIE MARSDEN www.berniemarsden.com
DAVE MARTONE www.davemartone.com / www.myspace.com/davemartone
VINNIE MOORE www.vinniemoore.com
STEVE MORSE www.stevemorse.com
MARIO PARGA www.marioparga.com / www.myspace.com/marioparga
DAMJAN PEJCINOSKI http://www.myspace.com/damjan1
MICHAEL ROMEO (Symphony X) www.symphonyx.com
MARCO SFOGLI www.marcosfogli.com / www.myspace.com/marcosfogli
STEVE STEVENS www.stevestevens.net / www.myspace.com/stevestevensmemorycrash
ANDY TIMMONS www.andytimmons.com
JOHN WHEATCROFT www.myspace.com/johnwheatcroft

RESOURCES

GUITAR MAGAZINES

Guitar World
Guitar Player
Guitarist
Guitar Techniques
Total Guitar

ONLINE RESOURCES

www.alloutguitar.com
www.bluesjamtracks.com
www.guitarinstructor.com
www.guitarplayer.com
www.guitarworld.com
www.ibreathemusic.com
www.licklibrary.com
www.infiniteguitar.com
www.modernguitars.com
www.musicradar.com
www.premierguitar.com
www.ultimate-guitar.com

FURTHER EDUCATION

You might want to take all this a stage further—and these following institutions provide the best training possible:

US
Musicians Institute www.MI.edu   Hollywood, CA
Berklee College Of Music www.berklee.edu Boston, MA

UK
The Guitar Institute www.icmp.uk.com
Guitar-X www.guitar-x.co.uk
Academy of Contemporary Music www.acm.ac.uk
BIMM www.bimm.co.uk
The Academy Of Music And Sound www.theacademy.uk.com
Access To Music www.accesstomusic.co.uk

INDEX

A

AC/DC 9, 13, 71, 80, 80, 85, 94, 153
action 15
Aerosmith 13, 30, 110, 110, 157
Aldrich, Doug 175
Alice in Chains 102
"All Along The Watchtower" 160
"All Right Paul?" 72–3
"All Summer Long" 78
A major, key of 152
amplifiers 16
Appetite for Destruction 82
arpeggio diagrams 27
arpeggios 166
Avenged Sevenfold 38, 97

B

Bach, Johann Sebastian 112
Back to Black 80
"Bad Company with Angus" 94, 153
Bad Moon Rising 175
Baker, Ginger 108
barre chord exercises 66–9
Batten, Jennifer 169
Beach, Reb 169
"Beat It Jackson" 114, 172
The Beatles 71, 88
Beck, Jeff 127, 129, 173
bending 35, 119, 126, 140, 141, 142
    vibrato and 129
Berry, Chuck 8, 8, 132
Bettencourt, Nuno 169, 175
Black 116
"Black Dog" 107
Black Ice 80
Black Label Society 162
Blackmore, Ritchie 8, 9, 13, 92, 92, 112,
    164, 165, 166
Black Sabbath 9, 13, 38, 85, 90, 90, 91, 96,
    100, 111, 112, 151
Blink-182 104, 156, 157

"Blink on a Green Day" 104
Blizzard Of Ozz 112
blues scale 108, 109, 116, 117
Bonamassa, Joe 119
Bonham, John 107
Bon Jovi 9, 9, 157
Boston (band) 157
Broderick, Chris 169
Bruce, Jack 108
Buckethead 169
Bumblefoot 169
"Burn" 166

C

Charvel 14
chord boxes 25
chords 32, 33, 135, 147–9
open 61–5
Clapton, Eric 8, 108, 119, 126, 127, 129
C major/A minor scales 164
C major chord 148
C major scale 146–7
Cradle of Filth 14
Crate 16
Cream 108

D

Darrell, Dimebag 14
Dean 14
Deep Purple 9, 13, 85, 92
DeMartini, Warren 129, 175
diabolus in musica 117
Di'Anno, Paul 96
Dickinson, Bruce 96
Diezal amp 100
Di Meola, Al 50, 165
Dio 175
"Dirty Diana" 141
distortion 36, 85, 149–50
"Down to Panama" 98
D minor blues 151

D minor chord 148–9
Dokken 153
double–locking system 173
double stops 159
doubling 160
Dream Theater 48
Dunlop Jazz III picks 17

E

The Eagles 9
"East Wes" 161
E major scale 145–6
E minor pentatonic sequencing licks
162–3
E minor sequences 165, 177
"Empty Rooms" 142
"Enter Metallica" 116
"Eric's Sunshine" 108
"Eruption" 167, 175
ESP 14
Extreme 175

F

Fender Stratocaster guitar 9, 12, 92, 173
fifth-fret open-string harmonics 170
fifths 149
fills 76
floating position 34
fourths (double stops) 92–3
Free 72
Frehley, Ace 9, 13, 133
fretting 31, 161
scales and single–note lines 35
"Funk Your Motion" 110

G

galloping rhythm 96
Garsed, Brett 55
"Gary's Europa" 142
Genesis 167
"Get The Funk Out" 175

Gibbons, Billy 92, 167, 170, 179
Gibson Les Paul guitar 8, 9, 13, 82, 94
Gilbert, Paul 14, 50, 165
Gillis, Brad 171
Gilmour, David 119, 127, 129
G major chord 147
Good Charlotte 104, 157
Gottardo, Daniel 169
Govan, Guthrie 169
Green Day 104, 156, 157
grunge 102, 104
Guitar Idol 169
guitars 12–15
    buying 15
    how to hold 29–30
    setup 15
Guns 'n' Roses 9, 30, 71, 82, 82

H

Hackett, Steve 167
hammer-ons 52–5, 119, 120–3, 124, 167,
    177
Hammet, Kirk 14
hand positioning 31–5
harmonics 170–1, 174
headstocks 18, 18
Helmerich, TJ 169
Hendrix, Jimi 8, 13, 76, 119, 159, 160, 173
"Hey Jimi" 76
Holdsworth, Allan 55
"Hot For Teacher" 98
Howe, Greg 125, 166, 169
Hughes & Kettner 16

I

Ibanez guitar 14
Idol, Billy 141
Iommi, Tony 13, 85, 90, 125
Iron Maiden 85, 96, 97, 111, 166, 177

J

Jackson 14
Jackson, Michael 114, 141, 172
"Johnny B. Goode" 132
Johnson, Brian "Beano" 80
Johnson, Eric 119, 161
Jones, John Paul 107
Journey 157
Judas Priest 9, 96, 100
"Jump" 98

K

keys 151, 152–7
Kid Rock 78
King, BB 127
Kiss 6, 9, 9, 13, 71, 133, 156, 157
Kollman, Jeff 129
Kossoff, Paul 72
Kotzen, Richie 169
Kramer 14

L

Laney 16
Lange, Robert "Mutt" 80
leads 17
Led Zeppelin 9, 30, 85, 88, 88, 107, 130
legato 52, 55
Lennon, John 107
licks 119
repeating 130–3
and runs 175–7
and scale sequences 162
Line 6 16
Linkin Park 9
"The Loner" 142
Lukather, Steve 114, 114, 125, 125, 129
Lynch, George 125, 129, 175, 177
Lynyrd Skynyrd 9, 71, 78, 78

M

Macalpine, Tony 165
McCartney, Paul 107
major chords 147–8
major keys 154
major scale 137, 145–6
Malmsteen, Yngwie 13, 50, 127, 129, 164,
165, 166
Marilyn Manson 9
Marshall amp 8, 9, 16, 94
Master of Puppets 100
May, Brian 119, 127, 129
Megadeth 100, 166, 169
melodies 140–3
Mesa Boogie Rectifier amp 100
Metallica 9, 38, 85, 100, 100, 116, 117, 157,
166
metronomes 17, 41, 131, 185, 186
minor blues scale 136, 138, 151, 175
minor chords 148–9
minor keys 155
minor pentatonic scale 118–19, 120–3,
135, 137, 138, 150
minor scale 138
relative 156
Montgomery, Wes 161
Moore, Gary 129, 142
Moore, Vinnie 165
Morse, Paul 50
Mötley Crüe 9
"Mr. Hyde" 160
Murray, Dave 177
muting 35, 36–9, 82, 167
palm 38–9, 96, 98, 100, 116

N

natural minor scale 151
New Found Glory 104
Nickelback 14, 157
Nirvana 9, 102, 102
nodes 170
notation, standard 23
note bleed 130
note lengths 24
notes on guitar 20–1
"Nothing Else Matters" 157
Nugent, Ted 71, 179
Number Of The Beast 96

O

octaves 161
open–string harmonics 170
Osbourne, Ozzy 90, 112, 160, 162
"The O Zone" 160

P

Page, Jimmy 6, 8, 13, 30, 107, 119, 123,
123, 130, 163
"Panama" 98
"Paradise City" 82
Paranoid 90
"Parisienne Walkways" 142
Pearl Jam 9, 102
Peavey 16
Perry, Joe 13, 30, 110
Petrucci, John 48, 50
phrasing techniques 126–9, 140
picking
alternate 50–1
chords and riffs 32
exercises 46–51
scales and single–note lines 33–4
single–string 42–4
picks 17
Pink Floyd 8
"Play That Funky Music" 110
Poison 9, 153, 156, 157
power chords 32, 79, 135, 149–50
moveable 59–60
open 56–8
using with riffs 84–105
power picks 87, 89, 91, 97, 101, 103, 105
power slides 115, 125
practice schedules and diaries 185–6
Prince 110
PRS guitar 14, 14
pull–offs 52–5, 119, 120–3, 124, 131, 167,
177

Q

Queen 9, 71, 153

R

Rage Against The Machine 9
Rainbow 92
Ratt 153
recording oneself 185
rests 24, 45, 94, 109
Rhoads, Randy 112, 112, 164, 165
rhythm 41, 111
rhythm tracks 181–4

Richard, Keith 94
Ride the Lightning 100
riffs 32, 33, 134, 149
open chord 70–83
power chords with 84–105
single–note–based 106–17
"Rock 'n' Roll" 107
Roland 16
Rolling Stones 71, 94, 110
Rose, Floyd 14, 173
Roth, Dave Lee 174
Roth, Uli Jon 112
Run–D.M.C. 110
"Run To The Hills" 96

S

Sambora, Richie 9
Santana, Carlos 14, 142, 160
Satriani, Joe 14, 55, 55, 129, 169, 173
scale diagrams 26
scales 33–5, 93, 106–17, 134–43, 140,
150–1
scale sequencing 162–5
scooping 174
The Scorpions 9
Scott, Bon 80
Seattle sound 102, 104
Shenker, Michael 119, 133, 176
single–string picking 42–4
Slash 7, 13, 30, 82, 133
slash chord 153
Slayer 14
slides 124–5
Slipknot 9, 9, 38, 97
"Smells Like Teen Spirit" 102
"Smoke on the Water" 92
solos 135, 137, 139, 161, 179
songwriting tips 157
Soundgarden 9, 102
"Stairway to Heaven" 130
Steppenwolf 86, 86
Stevens, Steve 141
"Still Got The Blues" 142
"Still Of The Night" 125
strap height 30
strings 17, 21–2
bending 126

INDEX

control of 85
string skipping 133
stun guitar 141
Sum 41 104
"Sunshine of Your Love" 108
Super Strat 14
"Sweet Child Of Mine" 82
"Sweet Emotion" 110
"Sweet Home Alabama" 78
Sykes, John 125

T
TAB system 23
tapping 167–9
two–string 169
tempo 41
Thin Lizzy 9, 142
Thompson, Mick 9
thrash metal 100

three–notes–per–string patterns 139
Thriller 114
"Ticket To Ride" 107
Timmons, Andy 129
Top Gun 141
"Top Jimmy" 98
tremolo 14
picking 172
triads 85, 95, 98, 99
Trivium 97
The Troggs 74, 74
tuners 17, 19
tuning 18–19
relative 19

V
Vai, Steve 14, 55, 125, 127, 161, 167, 169, 173, 174
Van Halen 85, 98, 98, 153, 156, 157, 167,

175
Van Halen, Eddie 6, 9, 14, 55, 85, 98, 112, 114, 125, 129, 167, 169, 170–1, 172, 173, 174
Vaughan, Stevie Ray 119, 129
vibrato 35, 119, 127–8, 140, 141, 142, 175
bending and 129
voicings 95
Vox 16

W
"Walk This Way" 110
"Welcome To The Jungle" 82
whammy bar 14, 173–4, 175
"When The Messiah Comes" 142
Whitesnake 125, 175
Whitford, Brad 110
"Whole Lotta Love" 88
Wild Cherry 110

"Wild Thing" 74
Wylde, Zakk 50, 119, 125, 160, 160, 162

Y
Young, Angus 13
Young, Malcolm 80, 94

Z
Zappa, Frank 174
ZZ Top 9, 71, 92, 133, 167, 170, 179

PICTURE CREDITS

All other images are the copyright of Quintet Publishing Ltd. While every effort has been made to credit contributors, Quintet Publishing would like to apologize should there have been any omissions or errors–and would be pleased to make the appropriate correction for future editions of the book.

A = above, B = below, L = left, R = right, C = center, T = top, F = far

Getty Images 6 B-L Redferns Collection/Getty Images, T-L Redferns Collection/Getty Images, C-L Redferns Collection/Getty Images; 7 T Redferns Collection/Getty Images, B Redferns Collection/Getty Images; 8 T-L Redferns Collection/Getty Images, B-R Redferns Collection/Getty Images; 9 T-L Redferns Collection/Getty Images, C-L Redferns Collection/Getty Images, B-C Redferns Collection/Getty Images, B-R Redferns Collection/Getty Images; 14 R Redferns Collection/Getty Images; 40 Redferns Collection/Getty Images; 48 B-R Redferns Collection/Getty Images; 50 B-R FilmMagic Collection/Getty Images; 55 B-R Don Arnold/MagicFilm; 71 Tim Mosenfelder/WireImage; 72 Redferns Collection/Getty Images; 74 Redferns Collection/Getty Images; 76 Redferns Collection/Getty Images; 78 Redferns Collection/Getty Images; 80 Redferns Collection/Getty Images; 82 Redferns Collection/Getty Images; 86 Redferns Collection/Getty Images; 88 Redferns Collection/Getty Images; 90 Redferns Collection/Getty Images; 92 Redferns Collection/Getty Images; 94 Redferns Collection/Getty Images; 96 Redferns Collection/Getty Images; 98 Redferns Collection/Getty Images; 100 Redferns Collection/Getty Images; 102 Redferns Collection/Getty Images; 104 Redferns Collection/Getty Images; 107 Premium Archive/Getty Images; 108 Redferns Collection/Getty Images; 110 Redferns Collection/Getty Images; 112 Redferns Collection/Getty Images; 114 Redferns Collection/Getty Images; 116 Redferns Collection/Getty Images; 123 Redferns Collection/Getty Images; 125 Jun Sato/WireImage; 157 Redferns Collection/Getty Images; 160 greetsia@hyperphoto.nl/WireImage. Shutterstock 8 B-L; 10; 15 T-R, B-L; 16 C; 17 C; 27 B; 28; 70; 84; 85; 106; 118; 134; 144; 158; 185; 186. iStock 178. Seiko 16 T; 17 B; 41 B-C. Slinky 17 T-L, T-R.Stratocaster Guitars 12. Epiphone Guitars 13. Santana MD Guitars 14 L. Ace Amplifiers 16 B.